Birmingham Memories

The publishers would like to thank the following companies for their support in the production of this book

Main Sponsor

LDV Limited

Alstom Transport Limited

Asbury Brodie & Company Limited

The Birmingham Mint

Bournville College of Further Education

Copes Service Stations Limited

Ehrhardt & Hereward

Fircroft College of Adult Education

Kappa SSK

Lench's Trust

Nason Foster Limited

MacDermid Plc

Newman College

Osborne Office Stationers

PPG Industries (UK) Limited

Widney UK Limited

First published in Great Britain by True North Books Limited
England HX5 9AE
01422 377977

ISBN 1 903204 45 3

Text, design and origination by True North Books Limited
Printed and bound by The Amadeus Press Limited

Birmingham Memories

Contents

Introduction

Let us say a prayer of thanks for the work of WH Fox Talbot and his contemporaries who pioneered the art of photography in Victorian times. Without their expertise we would have to rely on word of mouth or an artist's interpretation of a scene to be reminded of what life was like in the days when our parents and grandparents were growing up. We would also miss out on the opportunity of enjoying a book such as 'Birmingham Memories', for it is a magical mystery tour of the last century that unlocks a nostalgic cavalcade of emotion and recollection that can be linked directly to the images and words contained within these pages. Inside the reader will find glorious photographs of those bygone days in our city, enhanced by text that is poignant, thought provoking and knowingly pointed. 'Birmingham Memories' is not a history book, staidly dealing with stuffy facts, but a rich and wonderful stroll through the days when Austin Sevens bowled along Corporation Street, men in flat caps went off to the public bar for a game of fives and threes and women rolled up their sleeves and dug for victory. Relive

those times as you leaf through the days when granny danced the 'Lambeth Walk' and dad slicked back his hair and put on his crepe-soled shoes and drainpipe trousers. Look again at the marvellous architecture our forefathers created before the developers of the 1960s decided that we needed utilitarian high rise offices, concrete flyovers and multi storey car parks.

Wallow in the nostalgia that we all have for coffee bars, restaurants and tearooms before the invention of the dreaded burger bar and polystyrene takeaway carton. Those were the days of vinegar soaking through the newspaper that held our fish and chips, of real ale slopping in a pint glass and a sewing machine whirring in the front room as mum treadled away as she ran up a pair of blackout curtains for the back bedroom.

But not everything should be viewed through the rose tinted spectacles that we all use to look into the past, because there are many occasions when reality must overcome nostalgia. How else can we learn from the past if we do not take note of the sadder times? Inside 'Birmingham Memories' we will look again and wince at the depression years of the early 1930s that

The Edmund Street to Dudley tram wends its way past the Grove cinema, 1939.

found families in need and wartime, when we lived in constant fear of the holocaust from the skies and the knock on the door from the boy bringing a telegram that only contained bad news. Then there was the austerity of the immediate postwar years when rationing and scarcity still caused us to tighten our belts. However, when we have taken those difficult years on board, how much more joyous the good years seem. That real ice cream, not your synthetic whippy stuff, tastes so much better. The crunch of the end of a crusty loaf in your mouth as you failed to resist the temptation to bring it home whole from the baker's is that bit more satisfying than the prewrapped supermarket fodder of today. The memory of crispy bacon sizzling in the pan, rather than being poached in its own water as happens now, comes flooding back as we return to days when lifestyles were so different. Have we really improved our environment with the passing of time? Perhaps so, but at the cost of leaving behind some of the sights, tastes, sounds and smells we would have done well to take with us and adapt, rather than abandoning them forever. At least in this book we can, for a while, turn the clock back, reminisce and, hopefully, learn from what we have lost.

Birmingham is our city and, whilst we might grumble about some of its modern faults, we must celebrate all that is good and great about the second largest city in Britain. It has a noble heritage as well as a vibrant future, built on a history that saw it grow from a Saxon hamlet into a city of close to 1,000,000 inhabitants. In the 6th century it was a mere settlement surrounded by heavy forest under the leadership of Beorma. His followers (ing) made this their home (ham) and, from the combination of these words, the name of Birmingham developed. In the centuries that followed the Norman Conquest the de Bermingham family held large estates and were lords of the manor until Tudor times. Henry II granted the town its first market charter but, although it had a good water supply, its lack of river transport meant it was cut off from maritime contacts, important in medieval times. Its importance as the major market town in the area, added to some smithing and metal working, helped Birmingham maintain some influence, but its population only stood at 1,500 in the 16th century. The Civil War (1642-51) and the industrial revolution that began 100 years later provided the town with the impetus it needed to make the transition from one of

Colmore Row in the early 1950s.

modest size to one of vast importance. With its easy access to coal, iron and timber Birmingham supplied armour and weapons to Cromwell's forces and, as the metal and gun-making industries expanded, fine jewellery and brasswork served a world market. Pioneering engineers, James Watt, Matthew Boulton and William Murdock advanced Birmingham's cause as a major industrial force. The population grew from 15,000 in the late 17th century to around 70,000 at the height of Victoria's reign. Joseph Chamberlain, the social reformer and radical politician who came to Birmingham as a young man, provided the vision that established the Victorian city centre redevelopments from which the structure of the modern city is derived. 'Birmingham Memories' will help all lovers of nostalgia fill in the days from Joseph Chamberlain's death as the first world war loomed through to the sound of Slade belting out 'Coz I Luv You' at the start of the 1970s. The reader might have lived through some of those times for which there are strong memories, but others may just be a distant blur. Then there are those that

are out of reach, but hark back to tales told to us at our grandparents' knee. There are wild celebrations for coronations, the grandeur of Snow Hill station and the majesty of the Great Western Hotel to be recalled. We have Shirley Temple to remember, simpering her way through the 'Good Ship Lollipop', and peep-toe shoes to be purchased from Day & Co on New Street. 'Birmingham Memories' is your personal magic carpet and Tardis rolled into one, tickling your taste buds for dandelion and burdock in a stoppered jar and bullseyes at three farthings a quarter. Unplug the automatic washing machine and get out the dolly tub and mangle, put away the Dyson and beat the carpet suspended across the washing line. It is time to dispense with Playstations and mobile phones, so pick up a hoop and stick or top and whip and have real fun. A world of nostalgia is just a page away, so what are you waiting for? Each one of us will find some different aspect of our past being reawakened, but we will be united in our sense of pleasure with all that is contained beyond this introduction.

Around the city centre

Today, if the camera was pointed looking along New Street towards the junction with High Street, the Rotunda and the edge of the new Bull Ring would be the main landmarks to catch the eye. But, in May 1937 the photographer standing opposite Marshall and Snelgrove's was more interested in catching the patriotism and anticipation displayed in the banners, chains and flags celebrating the crowning of a new king. The former Duke of York inherited the crown from his brother on 11 December 1936 and for six months preparations were made for the big day. Some of the work had been done already in the presumption that the former Prince of Wales would be the one to be sitting in Westminster Abbey upon the coronation

throne, so it mattered little to those putting up the decorations who was being feted as the new monarch. As it turned out, the nation was fortunate to get the king it did, though it appeared unlikely at the time. Edward VIII, with his friends from high society, plus an American socialite as his queen, would hardly have been the figurehead who inspired the nation, but his charisma and debonair manner might have had us fooled for a while. Instead, we got a shy, but caring family man who was supported by a determined, energetic wife. Together, they restored our faith in the monarchy as they worked ceaselessly throughout the war years in open support of the nation, whilst the ex-king remained in the Bahamas.

Looking down Colmore Row from a position outside the Town Hall, with the Council House in view on the left, the commemorative pillar and gilded figure of St George erected to celebrate the previous year's Coronation of King George VI can be seen in the foreground. Victoria Square, from where Colmore Row leads away northeast, was formerly called Council House Square, but renamed in 1901 when the statue of Queen Victoria arrived. The whole square was revamped in 1992-93 at a cost of over £3 million, but the grand old lady was allowed to stay in situ, though she lost the statues keeping her company, not to mention some of the fine buildings on the right. The continuous line of palatial, Italian style buildings along Colmore Row remain as a tribute to the classical eye of their creator and perpetuates the memory of the mercer, William Colmore. The road has had various names, including Mount Pleasant, Bewdley Street, Monmouth Street and the Haymarket. At another time it was known as Ann Street, after one of the Colmore family names, but adopted its present title around the time the road was widened in 1874. The Colmore family crest contained a design of a Moor's head, with 'col' being the French for neck to complete the link with the surname.

Where once two medieval fairs were held and street entertainers performed, the open air market at the Bull Ring in 1952 drew shoppers to the stalls and barrows, many keen to get their hands on the fresh fruit that had been such a scarcity in the previous decade. Citrus fruit and bananas had been almost nonexistent, regarded as a luxury for which umbrella wielding women wanted to poke out another's eyes. However, they were probably restrained by the influence of St Martin's, the original parish church built in the 11th century. It was rebuilt on the Bull Ring in the 13th century and further enlarged in subsequent remodelling. The tower and spire were encased in brick in 1690, but gradually fell into a poor state of repair until PC Hardwick undertook its restoration in 1855. The body of the church was restructured in 1875 and included some fine stained glass windows created by Sir Edward Coley Burne-Jones. He was one of the greatest of the Victorian artists of the pre Raphaelite school and was honoured for his work in 1894 when he was awarded a baronetcy. St Martin's suffered in the wartime blitz when it was badly damaged. Restoration work was not completed until 1957 and the church stands today as the sole survivor of this scene.

Above: The passengers waiting in the tram shelter on Colmore Row in 1935 would have felt like only so much cargo if they took in the signs above their heads informing them that this was a loading place. They were standing outside one of the city's busiest and best known landmarks that opened in 1854. Snow Hill station was part of Great Western Railway, the company that enjoyed being known as God's Wonderful Railway. Within 25 years of this station becoming operational it was dealing with 200 trains on a daily basis. Railway companies also built fine hotels close to major stations and the Great Western Hotel, designed by JA Chatwin, was added to the site by 1863. As the station was gradually rebuilt during late Victorian and Edwardian times, direct passenger access to the hotel was created. The second half of the 19th century was a time when Victorians began a great exodus from the districts in which their families had lived for centuries. The rail network provided them with the opportunity to reach other parts of the country formerly too remote or uncomfortable to travel to. That, added to the decline in agriculture, saw many rural communities decamp to the industrial towns in search of a better way of life. As this led to overcrowding, not everyone was pleased that the move had been made, but boats had been burned and there was to be no turning back.

Below: The coronation of George VI brought to a conclusion the most difficult time the monarchy had undergone for centuries. The antics of Edward VIII and the secrecy of the government had thrown what had seemed to be a stable institution, respected and revered across the Commonwealth, into disarray. The politicians slapped censorship notices on the press, preventing publication of gossip about the king's affair with the twice divorced Wallis Simpson, even though it was well publicised in America and the rest of Europe. When the news finally broke at home and the king abdicated, the country was divided in its sympathies. But, it came together in May 1937 as it joined with nations as far flung as Fiji and Canada, Tonga and the Gold Coast to celebrate the start of a period of royal equilibrium, once more. The flags and standards flying the length of New Street displayed the depth and extent of the British Commonwealth of Nations, as it was called until 1946. The name had only been coined in 1931, replacing the former British Empire, with all its trappings of subjects bending their knees to conquering forces. 'Commonwealth' had a better ring to it, implying a togetherness not seen in the days when our national forces and mercenaries employed by large companies imposed their will upon native populations.

Fluffy clouds in a blue sky scudded overhead as two women made their way along the garden walk on Colmore Row, heading away from Snow Hill and the former Bull Lane, towards the Council House and Town Hall in Victoria Square. As the 1950s unfolded they talked of the changes they had seen in their time as housewives. Off to do the shopping, little was different on the food shelves from the days when they had first set up home. But, when they got back to their semis in Nechells Green or Aston the changes in their lifestyles would be clear. Food was packed away into the fridge instead of on the cold slab in the larder and the Hoover was dragged out from the cupboard under the stairs. 'It sweeps as it beats as it cleans,' they sang, just as they had heard on the ITV adverts flickering away on the little black and white goggle box in the corner of the room. Wasn't it great when that second channel began broadcasting in September 1955, giving an alternative to the staid BBC station? Even those first adverts for Gibbs' SR toothpaste and Babycham were entertaining, but what a shame that radio killed off Grace Archer in a fire at Ambridge in an effort to blunt the impact of the launch of independent television. The housewives loaded the washing machine and gave a silent prayer for the manufacturers who had brought an end to Monday washday blues, reddened hands and consigned that infernal mangle to the museum.

Colmore Row was bathed in sunshine in 1960 as a Morris Minor made its way past Barclays Bank and St Philip's Cathedral on its way into the city centre. Remaining in production from 1948 to 1971, this reliable car, noted for excellent steering and cornering qualities, was the first all-British model to pass the one million mark in sales; surviving models are still cherished by owners and collectors. The magnificent buildings, contained banks, offices and shops, along this stretch of the road have changed little today. They are best viewed by ignoring the logos of the businesses on some of the ground floor outlets and raising your eyes to the first floors and above. The majesty and grandeur of the architecture is quite breathtaking, with the intricate relief work a fine testament to the artistry and expertise of our ancestors. They were built to be pleasing to the eye and as a celebration of the combined skills of the architect and the builder. What a pity that developers and planners in the 1960s did not inherit such lofty ideals and aesthetic awareness, leaving us with a number of concrete, steel and glass eyesores, the sort Prince Charles has been known to criticise, as he did when he called the extension to the National Gallery 'a carbuncle'.

On 30 May 1961 the dreaded bingo, that scourge of the cinema industry, had arrived at the Old Square, Corporation Street. Audiences abandoned Cliff Richard's 'The Young Ones' or Elizabeth Taylor's 'Butterfield Eight' in favour of clickety-click and Kelly's eye. Dancing at the Mecca would not last long either, swept away with the Kings Hall market and other buildings as the wishes of the car driver outweighed heritage in order to build the Priory Ringway. Kings Hall was built in 1887 as the Central Wesleyan Chapel, but the Mecca's history was more consistent. It opened as the New Theatre on 14 November 1883, soon becoming the Grand Theatre, putting on operas and Victorian melodramas that befitted this elegant square. The building, designed by WH Ward, went on to become the Grand Casino, but it is the memory of the Mecca that most older readers will want to recall. They went there on a Saturday night, dancing to live music without the need for mindless DJs, in back to front baseball hats, scratching their so-called music under blinding strobe lighting. In the dance halls of that time girls used a Babycham and an Embassy filter tip as their drugs, with ecstasy coming from a last waltz in the arms of a handsome boy who walked them home and stole a goodnight kiss at the front door, if he was lucky.

Above: It is hard to believe that this was once regarded as Birmingham's village green, for it seems a far cry from duck ponds, games of cricket and strolling arm in arm with your sweetheart under the leafy boughs of the spreading chestnut tree. The FW Woolworth store, on the left, was part of the changing face of the 20th century, long after madrigals were sung and maypoles danced around. The original five and ten cent store came across the Atlantic to Britain in 1909, opening its first branch in Liverpool. Within 25 years most major towns had a 'Woolies' as a fixture. Work on the new Bull Ring in 1961 would obliterate any obvious link to those days of yesteryear and the completion of the ring road, built in 1967-71, with its concrete bridges, walkways and underpasses, would remove any trace of the 1835 Market Hall, the large building above the middle of the photograph. Birmingham was granted its first market charter in 1166 and, despite the loss of the Market Hall, markets continue to be held at the Bull Ring Centre. The indoor market has 90 stalls selling everything from fruit and vegetables to carpets, whilst St Martin's, in the centre of the Bull Ring, boasts 400 pitches for jewellery, crafts, household goods and clothing. The Open Market has 150 covered stalls, mainly dealing in food produce.

At leisure

Above: Open terracing, no segregation of supporters and hardly a bobby in sight; that was soccer 50 years ago. The Taylor Report on football safety was a long way off as fans made their way through the streets on a Saturday afternoon to watch a game at Villa Park. There was no trouble in the ground or in the surrounding streets as rival fans exchanged friendly banter with one another. Youngsters wore their claret and blue scarves with pride, swung their rattles above their heads and cheered their heroes on to victory. At least that was the theory: the 1952-53 season was a mixed one for Villa, only finishing halfway up the league table. Although success was important, it was not everything as there was still the sheer pleasure to be gained from seeing the stars of the opposition trying to pick their way past Villa's wing halves. Wilf Mannion, Raich Carter, Tom Finney, Stanley Matthews and Len Shackleton are great names from the immediate postwar era. It was a thrill to watch them, for we had but one chance a season to admire their skills, even if they were playing for Middlesbrough, Sunderland, Preston, Blackpool or Newcastle. Little lads were passed down to the front of the terraces for a better view by dads who knew they would be safe until the final whistle blew. Then it was off back home to listen to 'Sports Report' as we tuned in to the other results and heard about the match against Arsenal we had just seen. The description usually bore no resemblance to what we had witnessed!

Above right: A club mascot, dressed up in a silly costume, is not a modern soccer phenomenon, but Aston Villa's 'Darkie' would have the Commission for Racial Equality suffering an apoplectic fit these days. Even Robertson's Golly, that we had all collected quite

innocently since 1928 by saving up our jam and marmalade labels, was phased out in 2001 in favour of Roald Dahl characters. Whether being a Willy Wonka or a Twit will have the same attraction for youngsters remains to be seen. When this game kicked off children were more interested in enjoying the exploits of the 'Famous Five' in Enid Blyton's books or Dan Dare, Roy of the Rovers and the Silent Three in comics like 'Girls' Crystal', 'Eagle', 'Tiger' and 'School Friend' than any political correctness. The 1952-53 season was a mediocre one for Villa, finishing halfway up or down Division One, depending

upon your viewpoint. Hopes were high when the team ran out on 23 August as the mighty Gunners from Arsenal were the visitors, but reality soon dawned when the final whistle blew on an away win, 2-1. Danny Blanchflower, in the middle of those running out of the tunnel, was an outstanding halfback who would captain Spurs to great success in the early 1960s. Villa had a good cup run, losing to Everton in the quarter finals, but that was not good enough for the directors. Manager George Martin, appointed in December 1949, had to carry the can and was shown the door in August 1953.

Just a sea of enthralled faces, not a designer soccer shirt in sight, hardly any members of the fairer sex and certainly no hospitality boxes and fine wines to entertain business clients at Villa Park in 1952. This was the face of football half a century ago, back in the days when footballs had laces and a skilful winger would cross the ball, laceholes facing goalwards, for a centre forward to head home. In the winter, on heavy pitches, dubbined boots hammered a ball that seemed to weigh a ton, in an effort to move it a few yards. Centre halves were in danger of concussion after a succession of headed clearances, but that was their job and they stuck to it. Players had a specific role to fulfil as wingers hugged the touchline, trying to avoid fullbacks whose sole aim in life was to kick them into the stand. Winghalves brought the ball over the halfway line before passing it on to inside forwards trying to create a chance for the centre forward to score. They all had their own niche on the field, just as we had on the factory floor. Every man had a place, but knew his place in the society that went with it. The soccer terraces held 55,000 for the game against Arsenal and you could guarantee that all the home fans had Brummie accents and the visitors a cockney twang. Support your local team through thick and thin, with none of this modern curse of following a side hundreds of miles away just because it has some glamour puss in its ranks. The Villa team we cheered on 23 August 1952 was: Jones, Parkes, Aldis, Blanchflower, P Moss, Dorsett, Gibson, A Moss, Walsh, Dixon, Griffin.

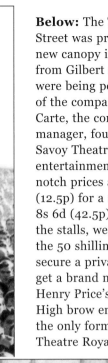

Below: The Theatre Royal, New Street was proudly showing off its new canopy in May 1953 as songs from Gilbert and Sullivan opera were being performed by members of the company Richard D'Oyly Carte, the composers' first manager, founded at London's Savoy Theatre in 1881. Top class entertainment demanded top notch prices and, at half a crown (12.5p) for a seat in the balcony or 8s 6d (42.5p) for the best seat in the stalls, were fairly steep. For the 50 shillings (£2.50) it cost to secure a private box a man could get a brand new suit from one of Henry Price's chain of tailors. High brow entertainment was not the only form that came to the Theatre Royal, as it hosted many variety shows. Mr Pastry (Richard Hearne) had audiences splitting their sides with laughter at his slapstick antics and David Whitfield crooned his way through 'Answer Me' before Sid Millward and his Nitwits got them chuckling again. The theatre had been in place so long that it came to be regarded as something of an institution, so there was hardly a dry eye in the house when the curtain came down for the last time on 15 December 1956. When 'The Fol-de-rols', billed as a 'song and laugh show and revusical comedy for high brows, low brows and no brows', starring Leslie Crowther, came to the end of its two week run, the cast joined the audience singing 'Auld Lang Syne'.

Wartime

John Bright Street was named after the Rochdale born social reformer who was Birmingham's MP for over 30 years. Built in 1881, at a cost of £31,000, it opened the way to the western suburbs, but today it lacks any influence, with its kebab house and bar either side of Lower Severn Street about all it has to offer. Pictured here, over 60 years ago, it reminds us when the railway system was one of the major targets for the Luftwaffe, as it provided the arterial lifeblood for the movement of troops, munitions and supplies. The raid over New Street station on 20 November 1940 also took out most of John Bright Street, leaving Severn House to stand forlornly surveying the twisted metal and burnt spars all about it. All night long wave after wave of planes pounded

Birmingham. Next morning, the army helped in the clearing up of the wreckage, a task that had to be repeated on countless occasions over the next nine months as Britain shuddered under the blast of what became known as the Blitz. We had won the Battle of Britain, when the RAF repulsed German fighter planes that late summer, but the enemy had learned the lessons of the Spanish Civil War, when resistance had been lowered by the aerial bombardment of industry and the civilian population. In September London bore the brunt of the first attacks, but it was not long before Birmingham, Liverpool, Manchester and Glasgow underwent similar treatment. Later in the war even provincial and historic towns were targeted in the 'Baedeker raids' on Coventry, Bath, Norwich and York.

Just another day at the office for the fire crew in January 1941 and the man strolling along High Street, near the junction with New Street, was taking it all in his stride. Sadly, Birmingham was getting used to clearing up after the air raids upon its fabric. It seems incongruous that the lonely sign, pointing to the ARP bomb shelter, withstood the blast of high explosive that shattered the buildings all around it. The bollard to the right, with its striped wartime markings to help drivers navigate during the blackout, has somehow come through unscathed. The same could not be said for the damaged remnants of the buildings in view, as they only seem to be standing in defiance of the laws of gravity. The same story was repeated across the city on many occasions during 1940 and 1941, in particular. Concentrated attacks were made on industry, with the Austin aero factory coming under fire in a daylight assault in November 1940. The BSA factory in Small Heath was burned out, with 50 workers killed in one incident alone when a wall fell upon them. The statistics alone are quite chilling, with 2,241 deaths, 140,000 houses destroyed and 654 public buildings flattened or damaged by the bombing raids. What the figures do not tell is the constant fear that we had and the awful sense of foreboding as the air raid siren sounded and the first drone of an aeroplane engine was heard.

The air raid of 10 April 1941 was one of the most devastating of the war, leaving the trio of women on Ivydale Avenue, Sheldon literally shell shocked. Even the workmen, making a start on clearing the rubble from the bombed out houses, seem stunned by the magnitude of the aftermath. One is so shattered by the experience that he just sits astride a heap of brick dust, too mentally exhausted to leap into action. That was how the scene affected many of those who had to mop up after the bombers had departed. To attend the site of such destruction was bad enough, but pity the poor souls who were first to arrive and lend a hand. They did not just have to cope with broken glass and falling masonry, there were the moans and screams of the injured and dying rending the air. In some cases there were body parts to be collected from the casualties blown apart by the force of the explosions. Putting little pieces of what were once human beings into dustbins was a job that provided nightmares for years to come, well after the hostilities ceased. Not everyone damaged by war received a physical injury, the mental scars lasted far longer. Thankfully, though we did not realise it at the time, the spate of air raids was soon to decline in frequency. Better defence strategies cut down the number of bombers getting through and, when Hitler turned his attention to the invasion of Russia, Germany needed her air support elsewhere.

Above: War is the backdrop for glorious exploits and daring deeds, the stuff of which heroes are made and the inspiration for great movies and thrilling novels. But, war begets war, for as fast as one conflict ends, another begins. We had not long recovered from World War II when Korea beckoned, to be followed by sabre rattling in Suez, uprisings in Kenya, Cyprus and Malaya. Then, it was off to the Falklands, the Gulf and the Balkans, not to mention over 30 years of civil strife in Northern Ireland. We even fell out with Iceland over a few cod! But, who really pays the price of all this turmoil? For the answer we may look no further than this photograph, for in that gaping hole is all that remains of not just a house, but a home. This was a place of laughter and joy, of happy memories where children were brought into the world and where grandpa and grandma came to join in with the festivities around the Christmas tree. On the mantelpiece were all the trinkets and souvenirs that traced family life down the years. Baby's christening photo, a coronation mug, dad's clock for 25 years' service in the factory and mum's china doll, won at the fairground in Llandudno, have been blown to smithereens. Worth no more than a few shillings in real terms, they were priceless to the family that lived here. As Pete Seeger was later to write in his song, 'Where have all the flowers gone?' - 'when will they ever learn, when will they ever learn?'

Below: Operation Petticoat was the codename given to the evacuation of our cities that began in late August 1939 and was in full swing on 1 September, the day on which Panzer divisions stormed into Poland in the blitzkrieg that threw the world into turmoil once more. Fleets of buses transported evacuees to the special trains laid on at New Street, Snow Hill and Moor Street stations, taking around 25,000 off to safe billets outside the city. The following day saw another 12,000 leave, some going as far afield as Hereford and Ross-on-Wye. This was about half the number that had been expected to go, but so many were loath to leave their homes or have their families fragmented, so they decided to take their chances and stay put. This same scene was repeated across the country as 1,500,000 children, labelled and clutching teddy bears and gas masks, went to who knew where. Few parents were given news of the intended destination of their children for security reasons, though the government promised to release that information 'as soon as possible'. That was too much for some mothers, who promptly removed their offspring from the platform and took them home. There was a clash of cultures for many 'townies' going to country billets. Receiving families complained about the dirty condition and foul language of the slum kids, whilst the evacuees were frightened by farm animals and moaned that there were no cinemas or pals to run around with.

Right: As the nation prepared for the inevitable war that was to be declared on 3 September 1939 people in high risk areas started the evacuation of the vulnerable to places of safety. The government was well aware that civilians would be targeted as the skies became a battle-ground as much as the trenches had been in 1914-18. ATS women, Local Defence Volunteers and the Army helped anxious women and children check the tickets they clutched and the name and destination tags worn around their necks. They were off to a place of relative safety, such as Stratford-upon-Avon, where they could avoid the carnage that would rain from the skies when the explosives and incendiaries were unleashed on their homes. At first it seemed to be nothing more than a little adventure or a short holiday, as many prophesied that it would be all over by Christmas. They had obviously forgotten that the same sentiments had been expressed 25 years earlier, but it took four Christmases for that conflict to come to an end. Invalids were amongst those chosen for the evacuation and teachers were included in the numbers so that children's education could continue out in the provinces. Not all the children were accompanied by their mothers and, for those who were torn from the bosom of their families, it was a tearful experience. Although some children were warmly received into new homes, others reported being taken grudgingly and having to suffer being treated as little more than skivvies.

Above: Throughout the war, the Women's Voluntary Service (WVS) collected clothing, food and other vital supplies to help those who had suffered from the shortages brought on by the difficulties of wartime. This was not a band of do-gooders, but an active unit in the civil defence. The women of the WVS were out on the streets when the bombs were falling, setting up mobile canteens and shelters for those made homeless by Goering's bombers. They supported the firefighters and rescue services, with little regard for their own safety. The organisation was set up by Stella, Lady Reading in 1938. Recognising that war was inevitable, the WVS ran first aid and gas defence classes for civilians and, after the war continued to give assistance in times of disaster, such as the East Coast floods in 1953. The service's flying food vans were ready to race into action whenever the need arose and here, cooking apple pies in Bluff ovens, members were on manoeuvres in the Civic Centre car park on 22 November 1953, practising their skills. These were nervous times, for the cold war with the communist bloc kept us aware of the threat of nuclear warfare and the need for immediate help should the worst ever happen. Men have always been involved in the service's activities and Mr RA Bashford, an emergency meals instructor, was there to lend a hand. In 1966, shortly after helping at the Aberfan tragedy, the WVS became the Women's Royal Voluntary Service.

Below: In 1938 we did not have a television in the lounge, one in the kitchen and others in the bedrooms, bringing us news round the clock. We had newspapers, but no moving images to go with them. Breakfast TV can now add to what we are reading over our toast and marmalade, but before the advent of the goggle box, people relied on the crowing cock of Pathé newsreels on visits to the cinema for moving pictures of world events. Additionally, there were the dedicated cinemas, such as 'The News Theatre', that specialised in shorts and film reports of current affairs, lapped up by a public keen for information about royal events and political developments. For a whole week at the beginning of October 1938 the same reel was run, extolling the virtues of Britain's 'greatest living citizen', Birmingham's own Arthur Neville Chamberlain. Son of Joseph Chamberlain, the influential mayor, MP and reformer, he rose through the party ranks to become Tory prime minister in May 1937. With the war clouds looming over Europe, he sought a peaceful agreement with the German leader, Adolf Hitler, in Munich on 30 September. His return to England, clutching the piece of paper that he said promised 'Peace in our time', is now universally derided, but to the public of the day it seemed as if the day had been saved. The newsreels triumphantly trumpeted the story, but it was a false dawn because the tanks rolled across Belgium and Poland less than a year later. Following a military debacle in Norway, Chamberlain was forced out of office in May 1940, dying a broken man six months later.

Events & occasions

It is no good being the mayor if you cannot enjoy a few perks of the job and few begrudged John Burman the opportunity of introducing his family to the royal couple when they came to call on 11 May 1948. It was the eve of the 11th anniversary of the Coronation and King George VI and Queen Elizabeth were happy to spare a few moments with the Burman family before their anniversary celebrations. Mrs Ursula Burman had made sure that her children, Elizabeth, John, Rosanne and Michael, had been washed, scrubbed and dressed in their Sunday best for the great day. They had been coached in how to bow and curtsey and in the correct form of address to use when speaking to a royal personage. All that protocol would have mattered little to the woman who was to become our very own 'Queen Mum', for she was a parent herself and knew that the best way to communicate with little ones was to act naturally. She threw off the airs and graces and chatted so merrily with the children that even her husband, an unsure and nervous individual, relaxed enough to be able to share a smile. It made the youngsters' day and, as they grew up, they were able to dine out on the opening gambit, 'Well, as I said to the old King and Queen when I met them...'

Below: The facade, designed by Richard Levin, announced that the land travelling exhibition of the Festival of Britain 1951 had come to Birmingham. A century after the Great Exhibition, mounted when Britain was the workshop of the world and the main influence on the industrialisation of other nations, a government sponsored sequel was held. Deputy prime minister and leader of the Commons, Herbert Morrison, was particularly influential in this display of national self praise. It was also a gesture towards a belief in a brighter future that inspired the conversion of a 27 acre bombsite near Waterloo into an exhibition site. The Dome of Discovery curved over much of the area, floodlit by the Skylon, a seemingly unsupported contraption - 'much like Britain', as one wag put it. King George and Queen Elizabeth performed the opening ceremony on 4 May 1951 in the structure noted for its texture, colour, curves and spaciousness. Further down the Thames a large funfair got under way and Battersea Park had an exhibition of modern sculpture, but pride of place was reserved for the only permanent building, the Royal Festival Hall. With its excellent acoustics and contemporary design, it was a success as London's long awaited new concert hall. The festival ran for five months, providing a welcome contrast with the drab air raid shelters, pillboxes and Nissen huts that were all that seemed to be built in 1939-45.

Left: People Travel showed the great strides we had made in finding our way across land, over the seas and in the air. It included this tableau, showing the interior of a modern rail observation car, complete with cocktail bar. Those passengers used to a diet of cold tea and curling sandwiches in the normal buffet car smiled a wry smile that British Rail had such a cheek as to imply that this was how train travel was going to be for people with second or third class tickets. The cocktail shaker on the counter and golf clubs in the corner let everyone know which group of travellers was being targeted. This travelling exhibition was a taste of the real thing in London, but it did give people unable to travel to the capital an idea of the sights and sounds enjoyed by those lucky enough to have first hand experience of what the festival director, Sir Gerald Barry, called 'fun, fantasy and colour'. The £8 million cost was not universally appreciated, coming in a period of postwar austerity, and was, not surprisingly, criticised by the Tory opposition party that dubbed it 'Morrison's folly'. However, the public turned up in droves, only finding fault with the cost of refreshments as it grumbled about paying 9d (4p) for a cup of coffee.

Above: The People at Play section attracted children and all those who wanted to relive their youth at the toys' display that included a model of a giant wheel, little trains and ships, plus an array of dolls and their clothes, over in the far corner. Vestiges of our childhood are always fascinating when compared with what interests today's youngsters. It is always a delight to watch some hardbitten executive turn all mushy when revisiting the toys from which so much pleasure was gained in the dim and distant past. How many of our great engineers owe their skills to the time spent practising the creation of bridges, cars and towers made from strips of Meccano and a few nuts and bolts? Did Britain produce architects and planners who had wrestled with the knotty problems of laying out a Hornby Doublo railtrack to maximise space or scientists who gave thanks in their laboratories for the days spent fiddling with the test tubes in their first chemistry set? If so, then there are those of us today who can look back as car mechanics who cut their eye teeth tuning a Scalextric car, as fashion designers who once cut a girl's figure out of Bunty, dressing her with the help of little fixing tabs on the clothes found on the next page of the comic, or as builders, proficient in the art of Lego.

The roof mosaic of the exhibition was designed by Eleanor Esmonde White for the Council of Industrial Design and was thought of as a busy, active piece of artwork. The discovery and design section celebrated many British achievements down the years, but most visitors were particularly interested in the most recent technological developments, particularly in television. The sets were expensive and often unreliable, with pictures that shook and often rolled around the screen, demanding attention from the horizontal and vertical hold buttons that required regular adjustment. Some cynics remarked that they would never catch on because radio provided all the entertainment and information anyone could ever need. By the end of the decade they had to eat their words as the television set became the focal point of most living rooms, even if you still had to draw the curtains to see the picture properly. The touring exhibition did the rounds of the provinces for several months until the formal closure of the festival on September 30th . It had been a good way in which to involve people outside the capital in the self congratulatory exercise of national pride. The government patted itself on the back at getting the message across to everybody that we had a land of which we could be proud. Unfortunately for Mr Attlee and his cabinet, the general public decided that this did not include their leadership as it went to the polls in a general election in October and returned Winston Churchill's Tories to power.

DESIGN   PEOPLE AT PLAY

Below: 'Vivat Regina!' they shouted, or words to that effect, on Francis Road, Hay Mills as they celebrated the 1953 coronation of Elizabeth II. How many of these little imps remember the day when they put on fancy dress as a clown, doll, Red Riding Hood or Mr Wishee-Washee in celebration of the 27 year old monarch who was to reign serenely into the 21st century, despite the various marital problems of her children that would embarrass her? Most of these children will be grandparents themselves by now, wondering if today's generation has as much fun as theirs did. After the fancy dress parade they wolfed down the party food their mothers had provided and joined in

games of musical chairs to the sound of Lita Roza's 'How much is that doggie in the window?' being played on a wind up gramophone. Down in London crowds lined the streets to cheer the procession of representatives from the far corners of the British Commonwealth paying homage to Her Majesty. One of the most impressive figures was that cut by Queen Salote of Tonga, a huge and beaming figure, who waved vigorously to the crowds as her open carriage rapidly filled with rainwater pouring down upon her. It was a good year to be British; Sir John Hunt's expedition had conquered Everest, Stanley Matthews won his FA Cup medal, Gordon Richards rode a Derby winner and the England cricket team regained the Ashes.

Bottom: Residents on Deakins Road, to the south east of the city centre off the A45 to Coventry, were celebrating in fine style on 2 June 1953. It was Coronation Day and the nation went wild with joy as the Archbishop of Canterbury, Dr Fisher, placed the crown on the head of Queen Elizabeth II. The weather was not the best it might have been, but who cared? It did not dampen our spirits, even if it made the fairy cakes and potted meat sandwiches go a little soggy at the street parties being held all over the land. The church hall had been raided for trestle tables and mums had slaved away over hot ovens to make the day that bit special. Fancy dress competitions were held and patriotic songs sung, rivalling the joyful scenes that were witnessed on VE Day at the end of the war. Union flags were hung from windowsills and jolly bunting draped from lampposts across the street as impromptu congas were danced on the pavement. The children thought the adults had gone mad, but that was not going to distract them from tucking into the goodies that lay on the tablecloths in front of them. The few who owned television sets suddenly found themselves very popular as neighbours crowded into their front rooms to watch the ceremonies being relayed from Westminster Abbey.

In the van-guard

How many vans and minibuses do we see each day on our roads? Anyone travelling along our motorways will see hundreds every hour. And even if we just stand at our own front doors and look out into the street it will not be long before we spy a commercial vehicle in one of dozens of modified body-styles making its way along the road. Where do all these vehicles come from; who makes all those modifications to what would otherwise be the manufacturers' standard output? One answer is Birmingham's very own LDV Ltd.

Bromford House, the international headquarters of LDV, is situated just next to the Birmingham to Lichfield railway line. The current HQ building was built in 1915 and for many years was the headquarters of Wolseley Motors. Although it is hard to believe today the site was once a

Right and below: *Devastating scenes at the Wolseley factory during the second world war.*

greenfield site; until the first world war Bromford House sat alone surrounded by fields. More recently, in the late 1990s, the building was extensively refurbished by LDV.

LDV are van specialists producing the widest range of panel vans and their derivatives in Europe; the firm's

ability to convert vehicles to customers' requirements gives it a strong commercial advantage over its competitors. Vehicles supplied by LDV are in daily use by discerning customers all over the country. Today the company has around 1,100 employees, most of them shareholders in the business.

The history of the plant goes back to the earliest days of the British motor industry. In the mid 1890s the general manager of what was then the Wolseley Sheep Shearing Company was Herbert Austin (1866-1941), a highly talented engineer and budding entrepreneur.

Herbert Austin, later 1st Baron Austin, made the first truly British-designed motor car in a factory just off Broad Street in Birmingham. Austin's early work led to the creation of the Wolseley Motor Company and in 1921 to that most famous of British cars the Austin Seven.

Very early in the 20th century the Wolseley car firm was acquired by Vickers, a company which even at that time was already a well founded industrial and defence conglomerate.

Vickers also owned a factory in Drews Lane and although there was some limited specialist vehicle manufacturing carried out there around 1912 it did not become a vehicle manufacturing centre until 1919 following the end of the Great War.

During the first world war Drews Lane became one of the largest munitions factories in the country employing tens of thousands of workers. When the war ended however Vickers no longer had need for such a plant and instead it moved Wolseley Motors from its Aston site to Drews Lane to allow it to expand its car production.

Between the wars Wolseley grew rapidly and was soon one of the leading British car marques. By 1926 with the success of the Austin Seven Wolseley was one of the leading car makers in the country, but it then ran into financial difficulties, largely through lack of product investment.

Another great name in the British motor industry, William Morris, (1877-1963) stepped in to save the company. William Richard Morris, Viscount Nuffield, had begun his manufacturing career with a cycle repair business; in 1910 he designed a car which could be produced cheaply and went on to build up Morris

Top: *Workers and soldiers at the Wolseley factory during the second world war.*

quarters of a million pounds from his own pocket for the Wolseley plant and manufacturing rights; he quickly re-equipped the whole site and introduced new models. William Morris spent a great deal of time at the plant and had a great affection for the workforce and their manufacturing capabilities. The new plant was so successful that Wolseley soon became the pre-eminent British marque, noted for its stylish and quality cars such as the Morris Flying Eight.

Today, in addition to vehicle conversions, LDV also manufactures automotive pressings and has a press shop which is amongst the largest in Europe. The press shops were built in 1937.

Motors at Cowley, Oxford. Morris was able to acquire great personal wealth and would become famous for his philanthropy.

Some of that philanthropy and business acumen would be directed towards Birmingham. Morris paid three

Top and above: More scenes of devastation at the factory during World War II.

In the mid 1930s William Morris had seen that his competitors were buying up their press panel suppliers and bringing the work in-house. Morris wanted to do the same but despite his millionaire status did not at the time have the ready money to spend in order to buy up an existing supplier. Instead Morris went to the government and persuaded ministers that if they would fund a new press shop it would be ready in case of war. The government agreed and paid for the new press shop - there is nothing new about government grants! Both Morris and the government had shown remarkable foresight. It is commonplace today to suggest that in the period right up to the outbreak of war in 1939 nothing was done to prepare for the war against Hitler and his Nazis. Prime Minster, Neville Chamberlain, may have been pilloried by Winston Churchill for his public stance of appeasement and allowing the reoccupation of the Sudetenland and annexation of Czechoslovakia, but in retrospect that condemnation was less than fair.

The truth was that the British government was deeply alarmed at developments on the continent. The rise of Nazi party Germany in the 1920s and early 1930s, following the birth of fascism in Mussolini's Italy, the horrors of the Spanish Civil war in the mid 1930s and the visible rearmament of Germany in direct contravention of the Treaty of Versailles were deeply worrying and the British had begun to quietly rearm. Possibly German might and aggression might be directed 'harmlessly' at the threat of Bolshevism and the Soviet Union, to the east rather than west, but it was surely better to be safe than sorry.

The almost secret investment by the British government in engineering facilities across the midlands and the north of England would bear an awesome fruit in the following years. When Hitler and his German hordes invaded Poland in the late summer of 1939 and Chamberlain was reluctantly, and sadly, obliged to tell the nation that we were once more at war with Germany the Morris Wolseley plant was ready to do its bit.

During the second world war the plant played a vital role producing pressed metal parts for the Crusader tank, Bren Gun carriers, parts for planes such as Spitfires, Lancasters and Beaufighters and virtually anything metallic such as helmets, fuel cans and mine casings.

Thousands of workers, many who had never worked in the industry before, risked bombing to work tirelessly to supply Britain with the sinews of war, material of all kinds which would contribute in every way to the eventual triumph over Adolf Hitler and his Italian and Japanese allies.

How many, now elderly, folk, look back at those years and recall their work at the factory during those days of destiny when each piece of metal pressed and shaped by machines guided by their hands could have meant the difference between life and death for some soldier, sailor or airman

Below: *Crude wartime catering facilities.*

famous remark that we'd never had it so good he was absolutely right.

Demand for every kind of product, perhaps with the exception of black-out curtains, was outstripping supply. And yet despite that buoyant economy, as the 1960s dawned, there were new clouds on the horizon.

The second world war might by now have begun fading into history but there were new kinds of war to be fought and won. This time the wars were commercial. The British motor industry faced threats from many quarters: the well established American giants, the ever present European car and vehicle manufacturers, and the nascent Japanese industry just beginning to put out feelers outside its own domestic market - an as yet still sleeping giant which within two decades would come to dominate the world market. And nor was that the only war being fought; domestically in boardrooms up and down the country corporate battles and deals were being brokered to push British vehicle manufacturers into ever larger conglomerates in the hope of taking what had once been a profitable industry back to its halcyon days. What was the problem? Some blamed the trades unions for demanding ever higher wages for less work. The workers by contrast pointed to the deplorable lack of investment.

fighting to save the world from the tyranny of Nazism? The knowledge that what they did might make a vital contribution to the outcome of the war, and perhaps even save the life of a loved one, certainly made peoples' attitude to their jobs rather different than it would be in less stressful times.

After the second world war William Morris continued to build up a huge industrial empire, he began manufacturing and painting van bodies for the new J-type van in 1946 - the real start of the van making tradition at Drews Lane. The painted van bodies were then transferred to the Adderley Park plant for final assembly and trim.

Before the plant began to eventually specialise in vans however there was other work to do. Body parts were made for many vehicles. 1.6 million body shells were pressed assembled and painted at the plant before going elsewhere for trim and final assembly. Famous bodies made on the site were the 1100 and 1300 series, the Austin Gypsy and the Metro 6R4 Rally Car.

The end of the war had brought with it a slow but sustained economic boom. The unemployment of the 1930s had by now given way to what was for all practical purposes full employment. Famously a man could walk out of one job at the morning teabreak and have another one before lunchtime. By the late 1950s when Harold Macmillan made his

Whatever the true reason, perhaps a little from both sides of the argument, the British-owned car industry began to

Above: *Home Office inspection of munitions.*
Right: *The result of enemy bombing.*

look ever shakier and the solution was seen to be to bundle most of the remaining industry under the single ownership of the nationalised British Leyland, later BL and more latterly Rover.

In 1981 Freight Rover Vans was formed as part of the then British Leyland conglomerate. That might have been the end of the story had BL been more successful. In 1987 in a move towards further rationalisation what had by then become the Rover Group disposed of the assets of Freight Rover Vans, along with Leyland Trucks to DAF BV of Holland.

By then the financial folly which had characterised the 1960s and most of the 1970s had dissipated. A new financial realism had descended across the world with Margaret Thatcher and Ronald Reagan taking the lead to ensure the capitalism and the sound commercial principles which underpin it would drive forward economic growth across the global markets.

Within that brave new world, and now part of DAF, workers at Drews lane might have expected their future to be bright. Alas it was not to be: just six years after been acquired by DAF disaster struck.

In February 1993 DAF in Holland sought protective administration because it had over-committed itself financially through making huge investments in new trucks and vans at a time when the European commercial vehicle market was in serious recession.

As a result the UK operation which traded under the Leyland DAF banner went into receivership and the future looked extremely bleak for the Birmingham site. Very quickly senior managers, led by the Chief

Above: *Staff and officials examining the havoc caused by the relentless enemy bombing campaigns.*

The 'Pilot' was also launched in 1996 and comes as a van, a chassis cab, a pick-up or a drop side from 2.2 to 2.8 tonne.

The Convoy 3.5 tonne tipper illustrates very well how the company produces specialist vehicles across the range. These vehicles are fully manufactured on-site ready for customer use. No other manufacturer offers such a level of factory service; if customers buy from a competitor they have to order the basic chassis cab and then have the specialist body made and fitted by a third party. This can lead to time delays in getting the vehicle into service and quality, paint and warranty problems. They don't have that with LDV! It is what gives LDV a major competitive advantage over larger European manufacturers.

The Special Vehicle Operations workshop is where much of the work tailored to customers' needs is done. All kinds of work

Executive Allan Amey, put together a plan to get the plant back into production. This was achieved within ten days of the receivership occurring and the management team quickly followed this with their own proposals to buy the assets of the company.

Managers successfully bought the company in a financing package of around £40 million. The deal was completed in just over ten weeks, a record for buying a complex company out of receivership. LDV Ltd began trading in April 1993. No longer a subsidiary in some much larger conglomerate the firm would thrive, helped in part by the fact that many employees would own shares in the new company.

Thanks to William Morris' farsightedness the plant had one of the largest press shops in Europe which not only underpinned van production but would also supplied Landrover with panels for its Defender and Discovery models. In 1996 a brand new transfer press line was commissioned

Most of the current volume is made up of the 'Convoy'. The Convoy was launched in 1996 and is available in many different body styles from 2.8 tonne to 4.1 tonne: vans, high roof vans, dropsides, chassis cabs, crew cabs; all available in short wheelbase, long wheelbase or extra long wheelbase layout.

is undertaken: a specially bodied laundry van for example which was built for Rentokil Initial has a design which improved the driver's productivity by some 40 per cent; this kind of service is only available from LDV.

LDV has constantly worked to improve the products it offers to both retail and fleet customers alike. In 1998 it introduced the LDV Club a new van based on an MPV (multi-purpose vehicle) design. This marque would boost the company's penetration of the retail and small fleet

This page: *Van manufacture in the early 1970s.*

sectors and would also prove popular with police forces. One area of the market which LDV dominates is the minibus sector. Thanks to a thorough understanding of customers' needs LDV has today secured around 65 per cent of the market in Britain.

With outstanding product specification: 17 seats - all with three point belts, twin rear wheels and spacious accommodation LDV has met the growing needs of the customer. And for specialist users such as schools and charities the company has devised a marketing package which is second to none and which includes attractive on the road prices, RoSPA advanced driving instruction for teachers, special insurance deals and low cost finance.

LDV was the first manufacturer to fit seat belts in minibuses as a factory standard back in 1992 and just two years later it again led the market with the introduction of

three point seat belts. Meeting the customers' needs has ensured that the company has stayed ahead in this very competitive sector. In 1998 it launched the new Schools Minibus which brought together a wealth of safety features after two years of customer research in

schools throughout the country.

By the dawn of the millennium a new £35 million paintshop was near completion, part of a £180 million investment programme in facilities for a whole new range of vans. LDV's Special Vehicle Operations business (SVO) continues to provide one of the widest range of ex-factory conversions and options in Europe.

LDV vans are in use daily by the Royal Mail, Parcelforce, British gas, Business Express, the Royal Airforce, the AA, British car Rentals, Rentokil Initial, Anglian Home improvements, the police and ambulance services as well as local authorities and fleet customers around the UK.

The year 2000 was an excellent one for sales with LDV selling 15,015 vehicles, an increase of 6.5 per cent on the previous year. And unlike its competitors LDV's market share remained consistent closing 2000 at 10.1 per cent.

Since its 'birth' in 1993 LDV has continued to be nominated for awards - and to win them. 2000 saw LDV gain further recognition with What Van? Minibus of the Year, and a nomination for Concept Vehicle of the year at the International British Motor Show. LDV has recently won two further awards Green fleet Manufacturer of the Year and the Fleet World Honours Environment Award.

Although the name may have changed over the decades LDV's roots in Birmingham now go back more than a century. The company's story has lasted from the late Victorian age and the entrepreneurism of Herbert Austin through many changes and crises to today's business world and the challenge of meeting customers needs in the 21st century - and though the names may have changed this at least is one firm that now seems eternal.

Top right: A van nearing completion on the production line. Above left: A van being sprayed. Left: Vans being prepared for delivery in the workshop.

On the move

Top: Corporation Street, in the late 1940s, gives little evidence to support the theory that petrol rationing was still in force and private motoring too expensive for the general public. The line of parked cars, vans going this way and that and vehicles dodging in and out of the path of the oncoming trams suggest that some Birmingham folk had managed to eke out their coupons well, or perhaps they had good contacts on the black market. Seeing such a jam so many years ago, no wonder something had to be done about the congestion in the city centre or things would have ground to a halt in a state of permanent gridlock. They were dangerous times to be behind the wheel as traffic weaved its ever impatient way along the highway, taking a chance crossing the tramlines made slippery in the rain. All these vehicles could enjoy themselves only for so long, until restrictions and pedestrianised areas were imposed on parts of the city centre. In the foreground, a dray just made it into the photographer's viewfinder. Brewing has long been an important part of Birmingham's economy, but we cannot make out from this picture whose fine ale is contained within the casks. Perhaps it belonged to Mitchell and Butler, now part of the Bass empire, an excellent company based at Cape Hill since its first brew bubbled forth in July 1879.

Above: George Formby, starring in 'It's in the air' at the Grove in Smethwick in 1939, was one of two Lancastrian variety stars who achieved the distinction of packing theatres with a stage act and filling cinemas when headlining box office hits. He and Gracie Fields reigned supreme throughout the 30s and 40s, continuing to play to full houses even in their later years, by which time they had become national institutions. With his little ukelele in his hand, George was the master of cheeky songs and gormless buffoonery. 'It's in the air' was one of his typical comedies, the story of an amiable, but accident prone RAF recruit. Audiences travelling on the Edmund Street to Dudley tram to watch his movie would soon have to use alternative transport, for the line closed in September 1939. This was not the end for the region's tram service because the last cars did not roll out of the Miller Street depot until 4 July 1953, when the last runs were made on the Short Heath, Pype Hayes and Erdington routes. Large crowds gathered, hoping for the chance to say that they had been on board when the final journey was made, but the opportunity came to few of them as the last car was filled with employees from the Transport Department. For them it was a case of 'turned out nice again', as George might have put it.

Bottom: Snow Hill station can never recover the grandeur of the days when it was linked with the Great Western Hotel alongside. It still functions as a rail link, but with far reduced influence. With the electrification of the New Street to Euston line at the start of the 1960s, the death knell for Snow Hill slowly sounded and it closed to passenger traffic in 1972. By then the hotel had gone and the whole station complex was finally demolished in 1977, the site becoming a car park. The revived Snow Hill is a mere shadow of its former glory, as then mighty locomotives filled the platforms and even the concourse with billowing clouds of steam. This was the beginning of the main GWR line to Paddington, rushing through town and countryside and giving joy to schoolboys perched on railway bridges, their notebooks filled with engine numbers they dutifully entered onto dog eared pages. Those halcyon days of rail travel, when services were smooth, efficient and, best of all, on time, are part of our history that we could do with bringing back. Modern commuters have become used to cancellations and delays, but we really did once have an industry that was reliable. Then it did not matter that passengers waiting on the platform could not understand a word the station announcer said, for there was nothing of importance to say. The train was there, ready to go.

Right: More than a Double Diamond was needed to work wonders on the traffic clogging up this corner of High Street and New Street on 3 April 1955. Even mixing it with a drop of Booth's mothers' ruin would not have provided a big enough kick to clear the jam that always seemed to occur at this spot. It was colloquially known as the Big Top because of the circus and fairground that were held on the bombsite behind the hoardings during the 1940s and 1950s. They provided much needed fun during the war and the hard times that followed, giving endless pleasure to young and old alike. In the circus ring the skills of the bareback horse riders, the performing seals tooting horns and the silly antics of the clowns were a great lift to audiences who needed something to cheer them up in those difficult times. Then there was all the fun of the fair to take in as well, with crashing dodgems and swirling waltzers, straddled by darkly handsome and dangerous young men swinging from car to car as they collected fares and flirted with

the girls. Over at the Wall of Death we squealed at the death defying stunts of the motor cyclists whizzing round the boards, apparently disproving all the laws of gravity. In the boxing booth young bucks tried their luck against the seasoned pro taking on all comers in an effort to win a few shillings and impress their girlfriends. They usually ended up with a bloody nose, but were rewarded with an admiring glance.

Bird's eye view

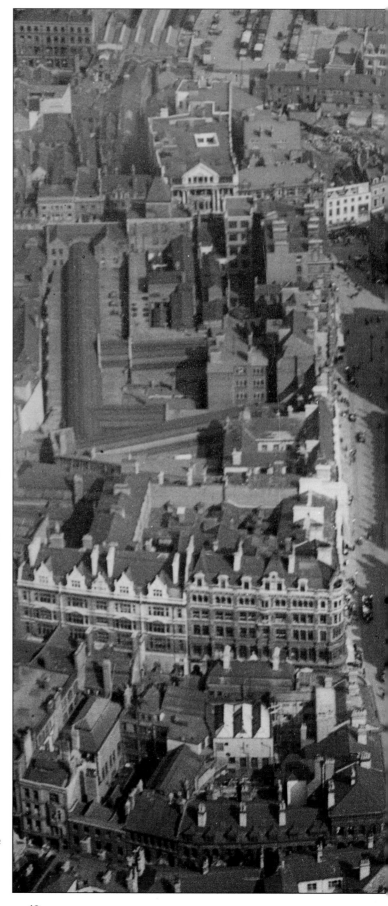

There was still roadway to see around the 1930s when this aerial view was taken, as car ownership was largely limited to the middle classes and above, but the time would come when such a view would show little sign of tarmac, just bumper to bumper traffic. In those days the railway was the main means for ordinary folk to travel any major distance. New Street station, on the lower right, handled thousands of passengers each day, going to and from work or off to the seaside for their holidays. The coming of the age of steam had not been universally popular, for those with conflicting interests saw the writing on the wall when the Stockton-Darlington and Liverpool-Manchester trials were held. Canal owners, seeing their livelihoods and profits under threat, blocked plans for a railway from Birmingham that would link with the port of Birkenhead. Protests were to no avail and, in 1833, tracks were laid to join with the Liverpool-Manchester line at Newton-le-Willows. The first train rolled out of the temporary terminus at Vauxhall on 4 July 1837 and a new era of transport began. New Street itself is one of the city's oldest thoroughfares with written reference made to it in a deed as long ago as 1398, when it was known as Le New Street. This must have been a mixture of Norman French and Brummie! Part of the street was once called Swinford, as a swine market was held there.

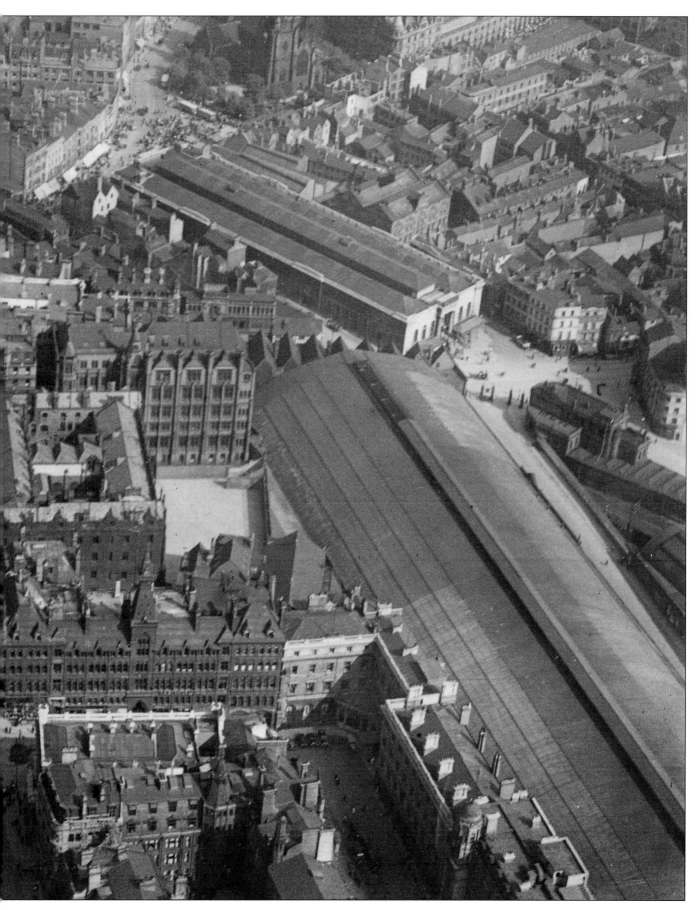

This 1959 aerial view shows the old New Street station, centre left, that was designed by William Livlock and built in 1894. It was shared by the London North Western Railway and Midland Railway, whose lines and rolling stock operated under a curved roof supported on 36 single span, cast iron arches, each weighing 35 tons. Bomb damage during the second world war led to the roof being taken down in 1945, though it was not until 1964 when rebuilding began in earnest. This was during the era of the infamous Dr Richard, later Lord, Beeching, the rail supremo who was given the job of modernising the network. His axe fell on many small stations and rural lines, but he did help some larger urban ones to modernise. He was sacked in December 1964, but his legacy long outlasted him. At least for New Street it meant that electrification of the line could take place and the modern station was further developed as its 12 platforms were linked with the offices and shops of the city centre. The modernisation took three years to complete, by which time British Rail had implemented much of the Beeching Report, slashing up to 50 per cent of its services. The great days of steam locomotives and an efficient and reliable network became but a memory. More recent attempts to improve matters, via privatisation and further rationalisation, seem to have made things even worse as the once proud industry has become a sick and ailing beast, best known for confusing pricing, accidents and delays.

In 1964 cinema audiences were enjoying the antics of the usual cast in 'Carry on Cleo', a spoof loosely based on the previous year's epic 'Cleopatra', starring Elizabeth Taylor and Richard Burton. The 'Carry on' regulars, who had us amused with their double entendres, included Sid James, Kenneth Williams, Kenneth Connor and Joan Sims. Also in the cast list was the luscious Amanda Barrie, a delight for any red blooded male to behold. She would later play Alma on television's 'Coronation Street', before being killed off in 2001. As the aerial photographer hummed the Bachelors' 'Diane' or 'Juliet' by the Four Pennies, he looked across the old St Catherine of Sienna RC Church in the Horsefair and along Suffolk Street, as it ran on to meet Smallbrook/Holloway Circus. The name of roundabout has nothing to do with the women's prison in London, but can be attributed to the 'hollow way' worn by heavy use in the old road to Worcester. Smallbrook is derived from Smalbroke, an old Birmingham family that took its name from a little stream at Yardley, the ancestral home. Horsefair was originally known as Brick Kiln Lane, but took its present name shortly after the fair moved from the town centre in 1812. The church was replaced later in 1964 by a circular one further along Bristol Street.

H ere we are looking down on the Gosta Green area, with the construction of what is now the University of Aston taking centre stage. It is one of three that the city boasts, if you include the University of Central England at Perry Barr. The University of Aston developed from the 1927 Central Technical College on Suffolk Street that helped pioneer day release courses for young workers. This scheme became particularly important during the war as demand grew for skilled workers. When peacetime came, Birmingham was designated the chief centre of technological development for the West Midlands. The college was, in 1956, Britain's first College of Advanced Technology and was promoted to university status in 1966. Its present site, in the triangle created by Corporation Street and Aston Street, is alongside the fast A38, as it becomes the A38M heading off towards the M6. The building in front of the university, on the edge of Lancaster Circus, was built in 1934 as Birmingham's new Fire Station. Today, the St Chad's and James Watt sections of the Queensway ring road intersect in a bemusing set of lanes, flyovers and underpasses, all designed to keep unwary motorists at their most alert. St Chad's is named for the city's Catholic cathedral, the first to be built in England after the Reformation. James Watt is best remembered by school-children as the man who sat looking at a kettle for his inspiration.

Birmingham is the United Kingdom's second largest city and one of its principal industrial and commercial areas. It developed from a small manufacturing town into a large city as it became the nucleus of the industrial revolution, though it was not until the Reform Act of 1832 that it elected its own members to Parliament.

The city was not incorporated until 1838, the same year that rail links to Liverpool and London were completed. But, Birmingham is not all commerce and industry, as this view, taken in 1967, illustrates. It has a number of interesting buildings, both modern and historic, including the Hall of Memory and Baskerville House to the left and the imposing

column of the 500 foot BT tower at the left centre. However, pride of place must go to those around Victoria Square in the centre, with its City Museum and Art Gallery, Town Hall and the Renaissance style Council House. The Museum and Art Gallery, built in the 1880s, holds its own treasures within, but the design of the Town Hall is its own testament to beauty. Joseph Hansom, of hansom cab fame, drew up the plans for the Roman temple style building in 1832, though it was not fully completed for 30 years. The Council House, built of the same Anglesey stone used for the Town Hall, was constructed between 1874 and 1879, to a design by Yeoville Thomason.

Many of the city centre's most notable landmarks can all be made out in this 1970 aerial view. Baskerville House is to the left, occupying a position it had held for 30 years. As the 21st century began plans were in hand to convert it into the Radisson Edwardian Hotel, with conference facilities, restaurant and leisure club. To its right, the domed building is the Hall of Memory, built of Portland stone at a cost of £60,000 to honour the 12,000 Birmingham citizens who died in World War I. Following a dedication service, the Hall was officially opened by Prince Arthur of Connaught on 4 July 1925. Further memorials were added after World War II, Korea, Vietnam and the Falklands campaigns. Local

artist, Albert Toft, provided the four external bronze figures that represent the Army, Navy, Air and Women's forces. The rectangle in front of the Hall was named Centenary Square in 1989 and now has the Repertory Theatre, Symphony Hall and Convention Centre at the near end. The building to the right of the Hall of Memory used to be the Municipal Bank, later LloydsTSB Bank. More centrally in the photograph, the colonnades of the Town Hall stand out, with the impressive Council House on the opposite side of Victoria Square. The Bull Ring's Rotunda dominates the scene at the top right, as it has since 1965 when it was built to James Roberts' design. It is on the way to becoming a Grade II listed building.

Shopping spree

The British are basically orderly people, accepting regimentation and instructions without too much fuss. Unlike our neighbours across the Channel, we queue politely, wait our turn and move along when asked to do so. The statuesque woman in the middle of this photograph looks something of a rebel, dressed in striking fashion that has turned a few heads, but she meekly accepts being guided across the road. On 18 August 1936 the throng in front of Dolcis' shoe shop was not fighting its way in to a sale, but was being instructed in new road safety measures at the special lights erected at the junction of Bull Street and Corporation Street. Bull Street, once named Chappell Street after the old Priory

Church of St Thomas, took its name from the Old Red Bull Inn, between Corporation Street and Dale End. Despite the smaller volume of traffic than today, accidents were too frequent for anyone's liking. Safety measures came in by the bucket load, with a driving test for all new drivers and pedestrian crossings being introduced in 1934. In the following year the 30 mph speed limit was imposed in built up areas and inventor Percy Shaw's cat's eyes were added to the white lines on roads that had only been painted there since 1926. The first automated traffic lights appeared in Leeds in 1928, but it took nearly a decade before they became commonplace. By then we also had pedestrian crossings, named after Leslie Hore-Belisha, the Minister of Transport.

Below: The crowds were out in force on Corporation Street in 1946, much as they are today as this part of the city has long been one of the main shopping areas. The view towards the Central Hall may have changed, now that the Queensway ring road cuts across by Old Square and Priory Walk, but the hustle and bustle is just as active. The very Corporation that ordered its construction named the street, somewhat arrogantly. It was designed as a rival to French boulevards, part of Joseph Chamberlain's grand plan to change the face of the city. Recognised as the founder of municipal government, he left the family's London shoe business to join his cousin in a screw making concern in Birmingham. His entrepreneurial skills and boundless energy quickly amassed such a fortune that he was able to retire in 1874 at the tender age of 38, having already become mayor the year before. Chamberlain's pioneer efforts in educational reform, slum clearance, improved housing and municipalisation of public utilities vaulted him into national prominence. The cutting of Corporation Street rid the city of some atrocious properties when work was begun in 1878, though it was not linked with New Street and Aston Street until 1903. By then Chamberlain had completed 27 years' service as an MP, being an influential and outspoken radical Liberal. He suffered a stroke in 1906 and remained an invalid for the last eight years of his life.

BUSES LOAD HERE FOR
BROAD STREET &
FIVE WAYS.
MOSELEY
3. HARBORNE &
   QUEENS PARK.
4. HARBORNE.
6. SANDON ROAD.
9. QUINTON.
12. HARBORNE &
    BARTLEY GREEN.

The one way system in New Street and surrounding roads was an early attempt to deal with the problem of traffic congestion. Even the man between the shafts of his own cart had to go with the flow. He must have been exhausted at the end of his journey, not to mention coughing and spluttering from the exhaust fumes he had been breathing in. Perhaps hay was on ration in addition to petrol or he might have had a pony to do the donkey work, if that is not a contradiction in terms! This was 1945 and petrol coupons were carefully eked out, restricting private motoring to about 50 miles a week, but concerns were obviously felt about keeping traffic on the move. Of course, worse was to come in the late 1950s when car ownership became more the norm and bumper to bumper traffic made our roads something of a nightmare. It is a problem that has never gone away, despite new roads and various attempts to persuade people back onto public transport. Back in 1945 it would have been hard to imagine a day when house builders made sure that new homes had sufficient space for two cars in every driveway. Then, our homes seldom had garages, so we parked on the street or some handy piece of waste land.

Above: Established stores on Britain's main shopping streets have come under pressure in recent years to rejig their image and represent the modern face of the 21st century. One of the most famous names of the last century, Marks and Spencer, has fought against the tide of falling profits, but not every major player has survived. C & A is the most obvious casualty of the last few years, something it could not imagine when it held a prominent place on New Street before it's move to Corporation Street. Handily placed by the Midland Red bus stop, it looks as if the passengers have, for once, ignored C & A fashions and gone to examine the bargains to be had at Milletts that, by the posters in the window, seems to be having a sale. If so, it would have a genuine one, held several times each year to clear out last season's stock and usually held in the New Year or around a summer Bank Holiday. Nowadays we see furniture stores and the like holding almost permanent sales, threatening that it all must end on Sunday, though they seldom seem to mention which one! Much of New Street is now pedestrianised or has restricted access, but it once echoed to the sound of hooves. Horse buses first ran from the Swan at Snow Hill and there were several hundred of these by the end of the Victorian age. On 1 June 1905 the Birmingham and Midland Motor Omnibus Company began operating with a fleet of 15 double deckers and the noble steeds were largely put out to grass.

This was a scene on New Street around the end of, or just after the war, for there are military uniforms on display within the ranks of shoppers going about their business and the wartime watertank was still very much in use. Hemlines are much shorter here than they were in the 1930s or early 1950s, a sign that precious material had to be conserved and of rationing, rather than any fashion statement. The bus in the distance would have been packed with passengers because petrol was a precious and scarce commodity, cutting down the number of miles of private motoring that could be managed. Corporation buses started in service on 19 July 1913 and

Birmingham saw an early introduction to trolley buses in 1922. This was unusual as most towns and cities brought them in to replace trams, rather than work alongside them. Another odd point is that the last tram ran in 1953, but the trolley bus had collected its last fare two years earlier. Midland Red opened its bus station in the new Bull Ring shopping centre in 1963, but the idea of malls and retail complexes was a generation away for the hordes on New Street. They crossed the road, moved from shop to shop, hunted down bargains and struggled back to the bus stop laden down with bags and packages. On getting back home there was hardly time to kick off their shoes before putting the tea on.

Above: On 29 July 1952 the market at the Bull Ring was in full sway, as the photographer pointed his lens towards the Osborne and Reading designed St Martin's Hotel, on the left. The scent of freshly cut flowers wafted across the open air market, intermingling with the sweet aromas of ready rubbed and Balkan Sobranie mixture coming through the door of Hawkesford's tobacconist's shop. Wheatlands offered the bargain of no purchase tax to pay on its furniture, in an effort to get shoppers to loosen their purse strings. In the years of postwar austerity it was not only the general public who felt the pinch. Shopkeepers needed to encourage sales in order to make a profit and keep body and soul together, but the rebuilding of both buildings and the

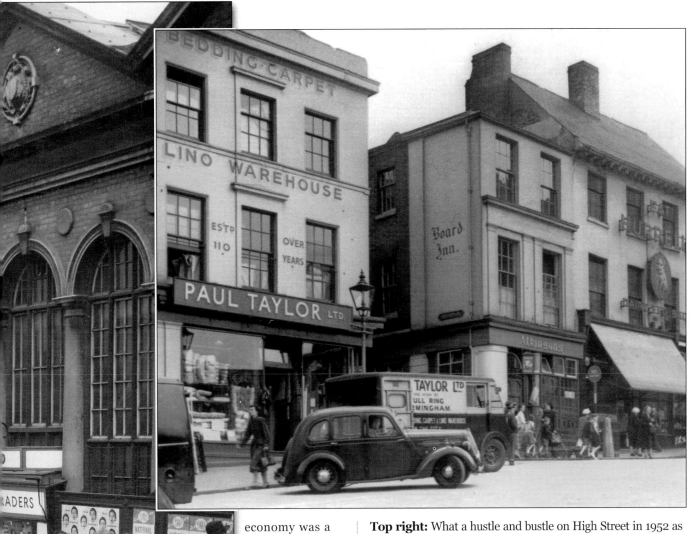

economy was a painful experience for everyone. Shoppers could get some light relief listening to the banter of the barrow boys and stallholders as they called across the Bull Ring with witty shouts trying to attract custom. They were not averse to chatting up some attractive housewife, but they were more interested in the contents of her purse than any favours she might bestow. Other amusement could be found in Woolworth's, where the girls at the till always seemed to have the stock phrase, 'How much is it, love?' whenever you presented an intended purchase to them.

Top right: What a hustle and bustle on High Street in 1952 as pedestrians and delivery drivers mixed together in the common purpose of doing the shopping. One provided and the other accepted what was on offer, for not everything was freely available. Rationing was still in force even for essentials, never mind luxury goods. The success of Taylor's lino warehouse bore testament to the way we had to be careful with our money half a century ago. Linoleum, that smooth surfaced floor covering made from a mixture of oxidised linseed oil, gums and resins, was trodden in most of our homes in those days. Hard wearing and easy to clean, it was cheaper than the wall to wall carpeting we have come to expect as standard today. Then we might have had our Axminster in the front room, but the kitchen and bedrooms would have been considered well furnished if they had as much as a rug or small square of carpet laid down. Heaven help dad if some stray ash from his Park Drive fell in the best room, even if he rubbed it in with his foot trying to kid everyone that it was good for the carpet. At least on the lino it was easy to brush up, but by then mum had probably chased him out of the house and down to the Board Inn for a peaceful pint in the public bar. This was the male preserve that women, other than the Salvation Army girl selling the 'War Cry', were discouraged from entering.

At work

Above: As World War II drew to a close, there were more than 2000 British Restaurants established across the country, serving cheap and, as far as restrictions would allow, nutritious meals to people whose lives had been disrupted by the war. Normal eating patterns had gone to pot in the air raids, varying shifts in the munitions and engineering factories and disruptions to family life by constant upheavals. The family meal at the dinner table became a thing of rarity value and the Ministry of Food took it upon itself to be the guardian of the nation's stomach. Here, an army of cooks set to work preparing as balanced a meal as possible, under the guidance of the government department, that would grace the tables of the Civic Restaurant on Cambridge Street. The tables and chairs were functional and so was the food, but workers got a main meal and pudding, washed down with a cuppa, for the more than reasonable 1s 2d (6p). Some of the ideas of the welfare state, introduced by the postwar Labour government, had their unofficial trials in the British Restaurants. Orange juice and milk for infants and schoolchildren, meals on wheels for the elderly and healthy eating campaigns all made their appearance under the guidance of the politicians, as they took responsibility for shaping our bodies as well as our minds.

After the armistice was signed to end the first world war the British government declared its intention to build a 'land fit for heroes'. Birmingham decided to play its part with a grandiose plan to build a civic centre in the area between Cambridge Street and Broad Street now known as Centenary Square. From 1919 the Corporation started to buy parcels of land around Easy Row and Broad Street. Architects' drawings and models produced in the 1920s show a series of magnificent collection of buildings around a central courtyard that included garden areas and a lofty single tower. By 1939 Baskerville House was the only part of the great idea to near completion. Work was finished the following year, by which time the country was at war and the remainder of the scheme was forever put into mothballs. The building is named for John Baskerville (1706-75), the Wolverly born printer and creator of a distinctive typeface that bears his name. In 1740 he set up a varnishing business, the profits of which enabled him to set up a printing house in 1757, publishing works by Virgil and Milton. He produced an exquisite edition of the Bible for Cambridge University in 1763 and is further renowned for a beautiful series of Horace and other Latin authors. The bold quality of Baskerville's print derived from his use of a highly glossed paper and a truly black ink that he had invented.

NEW CIVIC CENTRE EASTERN WING

Below: The conveyor belt at Austin Motor Company's Longbridge plant was in full swing in 1960 as Austin Seven body shells were suspended overhead, ready to be placed on top of the twin subframe chassis beneath. Car production began at the plant in 1906, but these cars being assembled are amongst the most famous in British motor production. The Austin Seven was a long running model name, dating back to 1922, when Herbert Austin developed his prototype in a converted billiard room at his home, Lickey Grange. Ably assisted by the 17 year old whiz mechanic, Stanley Edge, the first models they built sold for £225. As sales took off, increased levels of manufacture meant costs could be spread and the price of the cars soon fell to just £160. By 1939 other companies were basing their models on Austin's blueprint, including the first ever car to leave the BMW factory. But, it was with the involvement of designer Alec Issigonis that the Austin Seven's place in history was assured. He had designed the massively successful Morris Minor and, after a brief spell elsewhere, returned to what was now the British Motor Corporation. In response to the Suez energy crisis in 1956 and the popularity of Germany's Volkswagen Beetle, he introduced the boxy, inexpensive, fuel-efficient car that was, from 1962, known universally as the 'Mini'. By the time Issigonis died in 1988, over 1,000,000 Minis had come off the production line.

Above: By 1963 the car plant was known as BMC Longbridge, but many of the cars retained their traditional names, even though the British Motor Corporation had been around since 1952. It was formed by the merger of the Austin and Morris companies that also included Riley under its umbrella. Sometimes the dividing line between the old company names became blurred. This 1963 photograph is of the Austin 1100 that had been launched the year before as the Morris 1100! By the time these cars were reaching the end of the production line to receive their finishing touches, Herbert Austin had long gone to that great garage in the sky. He died in Bromsgrove in 1941, aged 74. As well as being an influential designer, he was also a member of the House of Commons (1919-24) as Sir Herbert Austin, having been knighted in 1917. He was made a baron five years before his death. William Morris died in the year that this photograph was taken, at the ripe old age of 85. Son of a farm labourer, he rose from humble beginnings to be made Viscount Nuffield in 1938. By then he had moved through the business ranks of cycle repairs, cycle and motorcycle manufacture to establishing his motor car company at Cowley in 1913. As his marriage was childless, he had no issue to whom he could pass on his fortune, so he turned his attention to using his wealth to help others. His philanthropic activities began in the early 1930s, beneficiaries including the Nuffield Institute for Medical Research, the University of Oxford, the Nuffield Trust, Nuffield College, Oxford and the Nuffield Foundation

Below: A man in a white coat looks more important and more scientific than a chap in an ordinary boiler suit. Standing like some conductor in charge of an orchestra, he was overseeing the work in the Longbridge body shop as private car production started to increase once more in 1948. Largely put on hold during the war, as attention was given to turning out vehicles for our troops, the postwar years saw normality begin to return, leading to the boom in car ownership in the 1950s. The success of Herbert Austin's business was developed from the experience the founder had gained with the Wolseley Sheep Shearing Machine Company. Whilst employed there Austin designed a three wheeler, Wolseley's first car, following up with the first four wheeler, the Voiturette. It won a 1,000 mile public trial in 1900, just the first of many awards that would come the way of this Buckinghamshire man who greatly influenced British and European light-car design. He set up his own company in 1905 and bought the site of a disused printing works at Longbridge, five miles out of the city. His first car was produced in 1906 and by the outbreak of the Great War he had a workforce of 2,000 making 1,500 cars each year.

A long tradition of looking to the future

The name Canning is a familiar one to Birmingham folk. Many will have walked down Canning Walk along the canal near the city centre since its opening in 1985 to mark the Bicentenary of Canning. It is appropriate that Canning Walk is very close to the site where a commercial electro plating was pioneered in this country and is a fitting reminder of all the associations the name Canning has for the people of the Second City. Over the years numerous of its citizens have been employed by the various Canning enterprises. Though these now go by the name of MacDermid plc, the industrial empire which was built up over a period spanning more than two centuries owes a significant amount to the members of the remarkable Canning family.

The Cannings, all of whom are related to George Canning, an able politician who was Foreign Secretary and briefly Prime Minister at the beginning of the 19th Century, can trace their family history back at least 600 years.

The company was founded in 1785, a time of historical and industrial significance. It was the year that Cartwright invented the power loom and steam power came to the cotton mills of Lancashire. National markets were being opened up by the transport revolution and there was a spirit of optimism and enterprise in the air.

William Canning was apprenticed as a fourteen year old schoolboy to William Gunn whose firm of druggists, grocers and drysalters (chemical suppliers) in Kenyon Street was to be taken on and developed with such distinction by William and future generations of Cannings.

*Top left: Founder of a dynasty, William Canning. **Above right:** Canning & Keates premises in the mid 1800s. **Right:** A Canning family outing in the late 1800s.*

An event of major importance occurred in the 1830s when electro plating on a commercial scale began in this country on a site very close to "Canning Walk". Canning was the local chemical supplier and so it was natural that it should be asked to provide the cyanides of silver and potassium, which were required for the plating of silver. The same basic process is still in use today.

Thus began an association of Canning with electro plating which is still the focus of the business.

Birmingham developed rapidly as the centre of the metal working industry, and electro plating became increasingly important as a means of providing a decorative and protective surface on base metals.

establishing it as a Public Company listed on the London Stock Exchange in 1920. The ability to raise capital in this way enabled the massive expansion between the Wars.

Canning became major exporters, naturally focusing on what is now the Commonwealth. Branches, Distributorships and Agencies were established in China, Japan, Australia, New Zealand, India and many other countries. This was the more leisured age of the steamship and telegram rather than air travel and the video conference.

Sir Ernest was the driving force of the company and was also prominent in the Midlands business community and local politics. This culminated in the Lord Mayoralty of Birmingham in 1938, and a Knighthood.

Canning made a major contribution to the war effort. For example, munitions are exposed to particularly corrosive environments and require protection; gun barrels are chromium plated internally to resist wear as well as the corrosive and erosive effects of the propellant gases. As in other industries, women were very effective in what had been traditional male jobs.

However, the post war years saw a gradual decline, accelerating in the 60s and early 70s. Sir Ernest had retired as Chairman in 1955 aged 79 (he died in 1966).

The company had lost its way; in an industry where the continuing income stream resulting from innovation in process technology was much more profitable than capital sales of equipment, Canning was badly positioned in having a large engineering operation, particularly as it was housed in old buildings unsuited to the production of modern plant.

A particularly important example of a valuable collaboration was with Joseph Lucas, who had begun in a very similar way to Canning, selling paraffin round the Jewellery quarter, close to the Canning shop. Lucas was a gifted entrepreneur who saw a market for bells for the recently invented bicycle. These needed electro plating and he turned to Canning to provide the means, both plant and processes.

This became a major influence on Canning as Lucas developed from a supplier of bicycle bells to become the foremost manufacturer of automotive electrical and braking systems in the country, with Canning as its preferred supplier. At the same time the Midlands established itself as the national centre of automotive Manufacturing which became the single most significant industrial activity.

This stimulated the development of Canning to provide the engineering plant, the basic chemicals and anodes, but most importantly, the proprietary process technology for electroplating.

In time it is the development of superior technology that has proved much the most profitable activity. But it was a long time before this was recognised. Initially Canning focused on the supply of the equipment and basic chemicals rather than chemical Research and Development. This allowed American and German competitors to seize the initiative and become the preferred suppliers of electro plating processes in the heyday of car manufacturing in the 1950s and 1960s.

Although Canning can trace its origins to 1785, the growth took place under one remarkable man, Sir Ernest Canning. He devoted his entire working life to the Company, crucially

Top left: Staff in the retail shop circa 1910.
Right: The Engineering Office, 1929.

Eventually this resulted in a takeover bid by an asset stripper in 1975; the "sum of parts" had become much more valuable than the whole. A sympathetic Government, concerned at the likely employment consequences, delayed the takeover until it ran into the sand.

However, this trauma stimulated a major reappraisal and reorganisation to the core business. Perhaps most significantly, the engineering and process technology activities were separated into different subsidiary companies.

Eventually the engineering activities were sold as a going concern, failed to survive and closed in 1981.

Meanwhile, the process plating technology activities, freed from the dead weight of supporting engineering, thrived and is the core business today.

Unfortunately, there were also some serious negative aspects to this change in direction. It was as though all the old activities were suspect.

The business embarked on a programme of acquisitions, seemingly without any real connection with the core business or coherent strategy. Most of these were failures, and there were heavy losses.

There was however one outstanding success. Marston Bentley was acquired in 1981 and there was a jewel hidden among its diverse product range; water based hydraulic fluids for offshore oil production. These fluids are used for remote control of the well head from the platform. The advantage over conventional oils is that they can be non polluting when discharged into the sea. The ability to discharge into the sea is very valuable indeed; leaks can be repaired when convenient rather than the system shut down straight away. This facility really matters when gales prevent divers repairing the leaks in winter when demand is high.

The demand for these fluids has increased enormously as land based oilfields become exhausted and the high cost of offshore platforms means that each one covers more well heads, with necessarily longer interconnecting hydraulic lines.

Canning has become the world leader in this very specialised technology. It has interesting parallels with the success in plating process technology as it shares the same success factors; leading edge "clean technology"; highly specified; niche chemistry; high technical service commitment.

Above: *Canning's very first Albion, solid tyred lorry, bought before World War I.* ***Below:*** *W Canning war workers in 1915.*

However, these two successful activities could not bear the burden of carrying the failed diversifications; Canning became vulnerable to takeover.

MacDermid acquired Canning in 1998. It was well known to and respected by Canning, selling a similar, but much wider range of processes, and indeed had licensed one of its electro plating processes some years earlier. It is headquartered in Waterbury, USA.

The major difference between the two companies, which had been of a comparable size in 1980, was that MacDermid had a successful acquisition record and a coherent strategy.

Canning, once shorn of the failed diversifications, was a very good"fit" with MacDermid.There was little overlap in those areas of technology where they had chosen to specialise; Canning for example supplied almost no processes for printed circuit board manufacture, a very important activity for MacDermid.

MacDermid have continued the belated investment in modern manufacturing facilities, which Canning had begun not long before the acquisition. All the MacDermid Surface Finishing activities in the UK are now concentrated on the Canning manufacturing site in Bordesley, Birmingham. Although necessary for efficiency, this had the sad consequences of the closure of MacDermid's factory in Telford and the historic Canning offices in Great Hampton Street, Birmingham. The offshore oil facilities remain at the Wigan site.

MacDermid have demonstrated their commitment by the further development of the Bordesley site, including impressive facilities for product development.

The MacDermid culture was established and exemplified by Harold Leever who exercised creative management skills and infused positive moral, religious and ethical ideas into the organisation. He established an ethos which had the interests of individual employees at its heart. The success of the company has been a natural consequence of this motivation. In his own words "When you do the job right, money happens".

Top: A Canning float taking part in a Birmingham procession seeking recruits for the brush factory, 1942.
Above: 20th Century technology comes to the Canning Research Laboratory in the 1980s.

Sliding smoothly through the centuries

A Birmingham company manufacturing horse harnesses and saddle fittings was the 19th century forerunner of the present day Widney company, which continues the tradition of manufacturing high quality essential accessory parts for off-road and passenger transport vehicles.

The firm Hallam, Sleigh and Cheston was founded in 1886 in Sandpits, Birmingham. Arthur Cheston was a dynamic personality with an outstanding record in sales backed up by a sound knowledge of engineering. Mr Hallam brought commercial expertise to the firm though, increasingly, took a low profile in the business. It is reported that he married three times and fathered 22 daughters, so perhaps his time was taken up elsewhere.

In the late 1920s the business was located in St Paul's Square, Hockley and was run by the next generation. Basil entered the business followed in due course by his own sons, Peter, Tony and Bill. They moved to

Above: A page from a pre first world war brochure.
Below: Launching a South African Railways train, which had windows manufactured by Widney.

Bagot Street near Birmingham city centre in the 1930s. The premises had originally been a cavalry barracks and had been the home of the Belgium Rifle Company.

With the advent of the motor car, interest moved from horse-drawn coach accessories to products for the automotive industry, such as locks, hinges, bonnet fasteners and similar items. The 1930s was a significant time for the company when it launched the 'Simplastic' glazing system which enabled a fully glazed window frame to be fitted directly to buses, instead of requiring screws to fix it to a wooden frame. The system was used throughout the UK and overseas so much so, that Hallam, Sleigh and Cheston were unable to cope with the demand and several of their customers made them under licence.

It was around this time that the company started to use aluminium extrusions to form round cornered

Both pictures: *Double decker buses fitted with Widney sliding windows.*

windows and the revolutionary concept of the sliding window mechanism was developed by Mr Oldham. Another profitable pre-war production was the bonnet hinge, which in those days was fitted from front to back of the bonnet, allowing each side to be lifted for engine inspection or repair. Virtually the total production of bonnet hinges for the entire UK motor trade was produced in Bagot Street by the firm's production unit Microvernier Ltd, which was located at Sandpits as a subsidiary of Hallam, Sleigh and Cheston. Another such subsidiary was the Widney Manufacturing Company of Maidenhead which was acquired from Frank Coward and carried on a blacksmiths business and wrought iron fabrication. Their particular speciality was headfittings for vehicles and after the Second World War they concentrated on London Transport windows which were Simplastic glazed as well as windows for rail and coach use.

During the second world war they undertook Ministry work, securing mainly naval contracts. This continued once peace was re-established as those were great days for the British ship-building industry.

Following the bombing of part of the Bagot Street premises during the second world war, Widney Moseley Hillcrest Works opened in 1940. It continued after the war to be the main manufacturing centre for windows. Following the end of the war the firm exploited the design of a telescopic slide which had been designed for the Admiralty. Slide production continues to be a large part of Widney's manufacturing activity.

In order to cope with increasing window orders from South Africa, Widney South Africa was established in Johannesburg in 1959, this was shortly afterwards followed by an incredibly high order from South African railways in the order of £1 million - a fortune in those days. The windows are still in use today on the Blue Train running on the South African Garden Route.

Left and top left: Production at Widney in the late 1990s. *Above right:* A 1980s Metrobus with Widney windows.

Hallam, Sleigh and Cheston became a Public Company in 1952 floated by Neville Industrial securities. At this time the Directors were AS Cheston, Chairman and Joint Managing Director, BM Cheston, Joint Managing Director, EC Edmonds, Export and H Whitehouse, Home Sales.

The company had numerous manufacturing premises around Birmingham; Plume Street was developed as a response to the requirements of the automotive industry and concentrated on the manufacture of seats, doorlocks, windshields and soft-topped canopies. Bagot Street produced telescopic drawslides for the Ministry of Defence and windows for buses and railways were made at Salford Street. There was also a network of associated companies overseas which all became independent of the Birmingham operation by the end of the 1960s.

Throughout the early 1950s and 1960s Widney had an extensive social programme, with successful football, cricket, table tennis and snooker teams. Whist drives and monthly dances were held to raise money for the social club which for many years organised a popular childrens' Christmas party.

The Bagot Street site was the subject of a Birmingham City Council compulsory purchase order in the 1970s and from that time all production has been centred on the Plume Street site. Widney was adopted as the company name, as Hallam, Sleigh and Cheston had

been selling products under the Widney trade mark. They were therefore well-known for product excellence under that name.

The 1970s saw major changes in the company. Martin Ferry joined the firm as Group Managing Director and Peter Cheston served as non-executive

chairman from the mid 1970s to 1980. It was around this time that they acquired two other companies in Cheltenham and Cirencester.

The sliding window mechanisms are still being supplied in great quantities and can be found on JCBs among other vehicles. They also supply slides to NCR cash machines. The company's particular strength lies in its ability to offer a wide range of products and the ability to design, develop and manufacture components to the purchaser's exact requirements. They aim to be flexible in their approach to design and manufacture and their products are readily interchangeable with other slide products. They manufacture a wide variety of telescopic slides solutions from small lightweight aluminium slides to heavy duty models with load capacities of up to 400 kgs per pair.

Products are manufactured using the latest technology including CNC machines, laser presses and a computerised 'shop floor' data collection system. They like to develop strong customer links so that they can have an ongoing evaluation of their products once they are in the field. There is a wide range of products manufactured including sliding windows, up and over windows and roller blinds for the off-road and passenger transport industry, as well as a full range of telescopic slides.

Quality is a top priority at Widney. The firm has received the coveted accreditation to BS EN ISO 9001 standard and is the preferred supplier to a number of major customers.

Widney's success has largely been attributable to its forward-looking approach and its ability to meet changing demands in the industry. Its adaptable development department is already seeking to anticipate future industry requirements and they are already working on the next generation of products. They will continue to stay at the forefront of the industry by combining their long-standing expertise and innovative mind-set for the benefit of their customers.

Left: Interior of cab showing roof hatch.
Above right: *Design utilises the latest in 3-D modelling on CAD.*

A fitting achievement

Walking through modern shopping malls and along High Streets up and down the country, how many of us pay a thought to the skill of those who have produced the attractive shop fronts and luxurious store interiors to which we have become accustomed? It is however thanks to the skill of firms like Nason Foster Ltd that these are possible.

The firm was founded in 1964 by Walter Foster and David Nason who had both served apprenticeships with Birmingham shopfitters. Wal met David after taking up employment at a shopfitting firm after he had completed his national service. They felt they had a special contribution to make and when it presented itself they welcomed the opportunity to go into business together.

Their speciality was shopfitting and high class joinery but in the early days they were glad to take on any work which presented itself to them, and they took on making fitted furniture, and hardwood and softwood windows as well as shopfitting.

They started out working from a large garage behind shops in Handsworth, Birmingham and then acquired a lockkeeper's cottage on the side of the canal in Perry Barr, and then a pre-war prefab behind it.

Having had a full training in all aspects of the job, both partners were able to undertake estimating, which they carried out mainly in the evenings as well as manufacturing items to fulfil orders and carrying out fixing during the daytime. After the business had been running for three years they were able to take on their first joiner.

They moved to their present premises in Moor Lane, Birmingham in 1971. At that time they took over part of a new factory and over the years have acquired more and more as adjacent units became available.

Above: Joint partners, Wal Foster, left and David Nason pictured in one of their workshops. *Left:* Company vehicles in the late 1970s. *Below left:* Kendalls shop front in the 1970s. *Below:* Ornamental fire doors and frames which Nason Foster were commissioned to provide for the entrance foyer of the City of Birmingham Council House.

NAS members are kept abreast of changes in legislation and customers can be reassured that products and services are designed for the safety of staff and customers alike.

There are over 35 people employed by Nason Foster and many of them have long service records. The firm operates an apprenticeship scheme so the tradition of highly trained personnel in the trade is continued.

It was only at this point that the partners took on staff to see to the administration of the firm, before this their wives had lent a hand part-time to do this.

It was a lot of hard work but they are justly proud of what they have achieved, especially their reputation for high-class craftsmanship, qualities which have made them in demand by such well-known High Street names as Burton Group, Natwest, Trust House Forte, Next, Suits You and British Rail. They were also entrusted with the commission to provide ornamental fire doors and frames in the entrance foyer of the City of Birmingham Council House.

The company has its own drawing office, estimating department and setting out department and joinery workshop. The drawing office is equipped with the latest CAD technology which enables the production of drawings and information which can be transferred directly to their clients via E-mail, similarly information can be transferred directly to their CNC machine thus saving valuable production time.

The firm has been a member of the National Association of Shopfitters for 27 years and David Nason has just completed two years as its National President, also over the years both partners have served as presidents of the Midland Regional Association of Shopfitters who are committed to promoting, training and supporting a full range of technical services to customers.

The new century is bringing changes to the company. In 2001 both Wal Foster and David Nason are standing back from the day-to-day running of the company. Though not ceasing to have the interests of the company at heart they feel they have earned themselves a well-deserved rest and are happy to entrust the future of the firm to the enthusiasm of those younger than themselves.. The company reins will be taken over by Peter Cirrone and Paul Sallis, both of whom have already given many years of loyal service to the company. They will seek to continue the tradition of excellence begun by the founders.

*Top left: One of the Next chain of shops. **Above left:** A store interior for Austin Reed. **Above right:** Part of the current fleet of vehicles. **Below:** Peter Cirrone and Paul Sallis.*

A friendly College with high expectations

Newman College of Higher Education is situated in the south west of Birmingham, not far from Junction 3 of the M5. It overlooks Bartley reservoir and its buildings conceal a series of inner courtyards and gardens that make the College a serene place at which to study.

The College now offers Coventry University degrees in a wide range of subjects. It was originally founded by the Catholic Education Service to train teachers for Catholic schools. This is still an important part of the College's mission but nowadays many students from other faiths, or none, also study there. The headteachers of many of the Catholic schools in Birmingham trained at Newman College and John McNally, Head of St Bernadette's School in Yardley, boasts that he has over twenty-five graduates on his staff. The majority of students at Newman come from the environs of Birmingham but others are attracted to it from other parts of the country as well as from Eire.

When first founded in 1968, with Simon Quinlan as first Principal, the College was a welcome addition to the area on its nine acre site overlooking the reservoir. There were some anxious moments as the day drew nearer for the first students to arrive. The then Archbishop of Birmingham, formally opened the College in 1969 but the first year students had to negotiate builders and decorators.

Newman College quickly established an excellent reputation as a teacher training college and many of the schools, both Catholic and non Catholic, in Birmingham have headteachers and staff who have trained at the College over the years. The College has hosted many famous visitors including Mother Theresa and Cardinal Basil Hume. Theology is one of the strengths of the College.

Newman College has developed an outstanding sporting tradition since its inception and has won many trophies for a wide range of sporting events. An international sporting achievement of note was during 2000 when the first European Universities' Football Championship was organised, supported by the European Union, the Catholic University of Leuven and the City of Antwerp. Football teams from 19 countries were invited to this prestigious event in Belgium. Out of 116 teams participating, the eight teams with the best results were invited to play at the finals.

The Newman Mens Football team scored 23 goals in their preliminary rounds without conceding any, thereby

Top: A Newman student enjoying the challenge of a field trip. *Right:* Students in the late 1960s.

Pamela Taylor, is also very proud of the excellent standards of support offered to its students during their time there. More recently the College has developed an IT Centre for local businesses and offers a range of training opportunities.

accumulating the maximum number of points in their group. In the Grand Finals, Newman won two further matches and lost only one, making Newman's final international ranking 5th out of 116 teams.

In the early 1980s, the College developed materials to help schools widen their expertise in computer technology. This remains a strength for Newman and they offer programmes in information technology for business, for the voluntary sector and for teachers.

Building on success in education, the College has developed courses in Early Years Education. Classroom assistants can study for a BA in Early Years Education Studies on a part-time basis. Over 120 are already doing so. The College won the 2000 NIACE Universities UK New Learning Opportunities Award for its Early Years provision and one of its students is the Early Years Practitioner of the Year.

In addition to the academic opportunities at Newman, students there also have the advantage of studying in attractive surroundings and they claim to be the friendliest college in the city. The site has not changed significantly over the years but the opening of the new Learning Resource Centre in 2001 will certainly give a new look to the College. The College, under the present Principal

Over the years Newman College has built up good relations with many of the universities and university colleges in the West Midlands. This, coupled with the well respected reputation of Newman College graduates, means that the College is making a significant contribution to the education sector in the local area and beyond. It is a reputation founded upon a belief that teaching children or working in the region's business community requires that gifted people are trained to a high standard. Newman's reputation is for warmth, care and high standards. It is one with which the Cardinal, after whom Newman College of Higher Education is named, would be proud to be identified.

*Top left: The Womens Football 1st XI, 2000. **Left:** Students rehearse a Drama production. **Top right:** Don Maclean, an Honorary Graduate at the Awards Ceremony in 1997. **Below:** An aerial view of the college.*

From physical training to vocational training

No-one familiar with the history of Birmingham can have escaped coming into contact with the philanthropic activities of the Cadbury family. The benevolent effects of this family has touched the life of the city at many points. The existence of Bournville College of Further Education is yet another reason for Bournville residents, and those from other parts of the area, to be thankful for this family who sought to put their wealth in the service of those who helped them make it.

It was in 1899 that Cadbury's, concerned about the physical well-being of their younger workers, decided on what was then a revolutionary step. They made it compulsory for all young workers to attend classes in physical education during working hours and teachers were brought in to instruct them. The scheme started with gymnastics but soon was extended to swimming lessons being given to their employees, young and old. The girls' swimming bath, opened in 1904, was a model not only for industrial organisations but also for many local authorities. A second bath was an outdoor pool which soon had many devotees.

The company toyed with the idea of compulsory evening classes but concern was expressed about the inadvisability of compelling young people to study in the evenings after a long day's work. From this the notion of offering compulsory further education to their young workers in firm's time was mooted and the concept of the day-release courses at 'Bournville Day Continuation School' was born.

The College opened its doors to its first eager (and some not so eager) students in 1913. The College remained a Cadbury foundation until the early 1960s when it was taken over by Birmingham Local Education Authority. But the Cadbury family has always kept up an interest in the college and has had a representative on the governing body.

It was originally on the village green at Bournville and remained there until 1972 when growth necessitated a move to the present building.

Today, the college is still committed to providing good quality further education but now it does not restrict by age what it offers. Originally it was young teenagers who benefited from the college. Now all ages may do so. Anyone from 14 upwards (that can mean 80 upwards) may take advantage of courses offered there. Those who feel they did not get a proper chance of a good education first time round can make good the deficiency with courses at the college.

Top: Mr CJV Bews, Headmaster from 1913 until 1946.
Left: Physical training in the early 1900s.

Students are drawn from a wide area round Birmingham, including Dudley, Sandwell and Worcestershire, but they are certainly not inward-looking. Over the years strong links have been developed with colleges in Italy, The Netherlands and France. Such links open up wider horizons to the college and offer their students greater opportunities for study and work.

In keeping with the tradition of innovation and being at the forefront of the educational race, the College appointed one of the first women Principals in the country. Patricia Twyman has been in the post since 1986 and is continuing the tradition of her predecessors. The college has already had a distinguished history spanning nearly a century. It will continue this tradition in the years to come by continuous improvement in order to achieve excellence in all they do, by building on its present strengths and by developing additional centres of vocational excellence.

Special strengths of the college include health and social care studies, as well as business and management courses. They are also keen to offer help to those with learning difficulties and/or disabilities of various kinds. In fact they are proud of the fact that they value all students and staff equally, regardless of whether they have a disability, whether they are male or female, or black or white, young or old.

Top left: The opening of the school by the Lord Mayor of Birmingham, Sir Percival Bower, 1925.
Above left: HRH Princess Royal's visit to mark the college's 75th Jubilee, 1989. **Below:** *Bournville College in 1988.*

The College is one of the oldest Further Education Colleges in England and is on an excellent site. They seek to form good relationships and partnerships with other colleges in the Birmingham area and recognise the value of effective links with schools. They pursue mutually advantageous partnerships with business, industry, commerce, the community and all other organisations linked to the college, such as the Local Education Authority and the Regional Development Agency.

From watches to turned parts

One of the great mysteries of life is why some of us are successful in our careers and others are not. Some people inherit a fortune and die paupers, others are born into poverty and are able to drag themselves up by their own bootstraps. Some men seem to have been born entrepreneurs and their ability to achieve something in their lives is completely independent of their family circumstances - they make their own luck.

Over on the continent in Germany in 1831 a child was born who would one day stamp his personal mark on the Birmingham engineering scene; he was clearly one of those blessed few whose aspirations are happily matched by their abilities.

In 1854 an adventurous 18 year old stowaway, young Wilhelm Ehrhardt, made his way across the North Sea from Germany to England. The young man would soon set up as a watchmaker in Barr Street, Hockley, Birmingham and founded the firm of W Ehrhardt Ltd. The company would become one of the first in the world to use fully automated machines to manufacture precision

watches, clocks, racks, pinions and gears. It also pioneered many new processes. Following Wilhelm's death in 1897 his sons continued the business.

The British Watch Company Ltd was founded in 1910 as successor to the original company. A year later Wilhelm's sons William and Gustav V Ehrhardt were made directors to carry on manufacturing, at what was now the aptly named Time Works, where they continued to make quality time pieces and horological equipment.

The company's name was changed once more in 1927 to GV Ehrhardt & Hereward Ltd, the first chairman being Ernest Francis Ehrhardt and it continued to engage in the manufacture of precision automatic turned parts, racks and pinions. The change of name reflected the involvement of other family members, namely the Herewards.

Top: Founder Wilhelm Ehrhardt. ***Right:*** *A fine pocket watch manufactured by the firm in the late 19th century.*

After 100 years at the same premises the firm moved to Vyse Street, Hockley in 1954. The firm would however only stay there for some 10 years.

In 1959 on the retirement of the managing director, Miss GS Reeves, the board of directors decided to sell the company to James Herbert Smart, chairman of the engineering company CAP Productions Ltd.

Jim Smart and CAP appreciated the firm's history and its good name in the trade; whilst acquiring the business CAP retained the original name within the CAP group as a producer of high quality automatic repetition turned parts.

By 1964 turnover had increased tremendously and the firm had moved to the present larger premises at The Crescent, Hockley. JH Smart's son Godfrey was by now guiding a large expansion programme of buildings and plant which would be completed twelve months later.

Today, led by Chairman Godfrey Smart, J&G Smart (Holdings)Ltd has evolved from CAP Productions Ltd. CAP was founded in 1945 by Birmingham born engineer James H Smart whose ideas of quality-driven efficiency and customer satisfaction remain throughout the group to this day. The independent engineering group now comprises

not just Ehrhardt & Hereward and CAP Productions Ltd but also Capco Presswork at Great Barr and Capco Palmer Steels based in Tipton.

The firm's standards and systems are focused on customer satisfaction in line with the edicts of the British Standards Institute. As a turned parts manufacturer multi and single spindle automatics are used producing medium and high volume components in steel, brass, aluminium and stainless steel. Drilling, milling and plating facilities are offered whilst precision presswork is available up to 160 tonnes; large stocks of bearings for multiple commercial applications are always available.

The firm's customer base is very diverse and includes the automotive industry, domestic appliance makers and the hardware industry.

Equipment has changed dramatically over the decades in the engineering industry, and computers have made their presence felt for many years now. However, although Ehrhardt and Hereward are no longer engaged in the horological industry, the equipment and raw materials used for watch making today still remain remarkably very similar to the tools and materials which Wilhelm Ehrhardt would have known. It seems at least some things can't be improved after all!

Above: *Ernest Francis Ehrhardt, the first Chairman of GV Ehrhardt & Hereward Ltd.*
Below, both pictures: *A small selection of some of the volume turned parts and pressings manufactured for Europe's industries.*

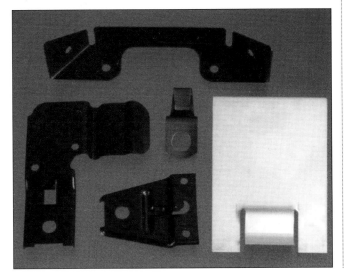

The benefit of trust

Something which crosses the mind, perhaps increasingly as one gets older is how will we be remembered once are no longer around. Few of us will give so much cause for gratitude as a certain William Lench, a tanner who lived in the early part of the 1500s.

At this time Henry VIII was on the throne and was causing complete turmoil throughout the country with his reforms of the church including his confiscation of church property and land.

William worked at his tanning trade in what is today called Moor Street but which went under the name of Mole Street at that time. Tanning was one of the principal trades in 'Byrmyncham' at this time. He along with numerous others made a good living from working leather and he invested much of his profits in land acquisition.

Things were going well for William and his wife, Anne but to their great sorrow they were childless and they were faced with the dilemma about whom they could leave their wealth to after their deaths.

After considering various options William decided on bequeathing his land to a Trust under the management of twelve of his most trusted friends. They were to administer the income generated by the land in The County of Warwick, the parishes of Dudston, Aston, Bordesley, Little Bromwich and Saltley for 'the necessitous poor of Birmingham'. William intended the money to help Birmingham townsfolk in two ways; firstly to go towards the construction and maintenance of Birmingham's bridges and streets. Many streams and

Right: *Conybere Street Alsmshouse built in 1864.*
Below: *Trustees and residents pictured in 1925.*

Today all the flats are self-contained and built to modern standards with well furnished and well used community rooms. The latest installation has a bathing room and the Trust employs someone who can assist those who find it difficult to get in and out of the bath. Each almshouse has a resident warden and an alarm system that enables even the frailest resident to feel secure.

The payment of stipends was phased out with the introduction of the National Health Insurance Act of 1948. But the trust still prides itself on providing good quality sheltered housing for the lowest possible contribution.

becks ran through the town and bridges were always collapsing. Street maintenance at this time was the responsibility of householders and many were not in a position to finance necessary repairs. The second purpose was to provide almshouses for the poor.

Throughout the last four centuries the Trust has benefited numerous people and still continues to do so today. Until 1838 when the City of Birmingham was incorporated, the income of the Trust was used for these two purposes. Since Birmingham became a city and the responsibility for street and bridges passed to them, the Trust has concentrated its efforts on looking after those unable to afford suitable housing. It also was able to give small stipends (pensions) to those in need. This was an extremely important provision for many, as State pensions did not come into existence until 1911.

The first reference to almshouses in the Trust's history is 1639, the Digbeth Almshouses. In 1688 the Trustees built another group at the corner of Steelhouse Lane and Lancaster Street in 'rural surroundings', with 'an extensive and beautiful view of the country'.

Since those beginnings the Trust has gone from strength to strength. The early almshouses have long since been demolished and new ones have taken their place. Today there are five groups of sheltered housing within Birmingham, two built during the 1860s and the newest as recently as 1993.

The values of the original twelve Trustees are still upheld today by their twelve successors, who are dedicated to providing a 'home for life' to some of Birmingham's elderly poor and needy. There is always a long waiting list for this accommodation.

The offices of the Trust are at 231 Hagley Road, Birmingham. The Trust has been administered for thirteen years by Jenny McGowran. She feels that William and Agnes Lench, as well as those first twelve Trustees, would be well satisfied with what the Trust had done throughout its history so far and what it continues to do today.

Top left: Lench's Close Almshouse at Moseley.
Below: Trustees and residents pictured in 1991.

From stations to stationery

With two dozen outlets scattered across the Midlands, Osborne Office Stationers is one of the most readily recognisable names on our high streets. But that could so easily have not been the case; a little over 30 years ago the company which can trace its history back to the reign of William IV seemed more likely to close down, than to grow to become today's multi-million pound business.

In 1832 Edward Corn Osborne, then 23 years old, established a printing business at 30 Bennetts Hill, in the centre of Birmingham, some thirty years later he would move to 84 New Street.

Edward and his wife Emily would have 8 children, including Edward Marmaduke Osborne who would eventually succeed his father in the business. The fledgling firm traded under

Above: Edward Corn Osborne.
Right: Edith Wynne, daughter of Herbert, pictured in the doorway of their Ethel Street shop, circa 1934.
Below: EC Osborne's premises in 1971.

the title of EC & W Osborne and specialised in producing information for the railways such as timetables and the authoritative 'Osbornes Grand Junction Railway Guide', first produced in 1838.

EC Osborne became a well known and respected figure in Birmingham being elected to the town council for the Ladybrook ward in 1856 and serving as Alderman from 1862 to 1882; he was particularly involved in the provision of Free Library Services; he was also a Justice of the Peace. Edward Osborne senior died at his home on Frederick Road, Edgbaston in 1886.

In 1914 EC Osborne became a limited company and in 1918 the family sold out to Herbert Wynne, then the manager of

Popes, the well known Birmingham stationers. The firm prospered under Herbert Wynne until the outbreak of the second world war. By now based at 6 St Paul's Square and with a branch in Ethel Street, the firm had a thriving 'own label' product range and had also moved into greeting cards.

As for so many businesses the war was a disaster, with St Paul's Square being destroyed by bombs. A move to Moor Street was not particularly successful and in the 1950s EC Osborne Ltd relocated to Sparkbrook in the suburbs and from there operated as a traditional commercial printer and stationer still under the ownership of the Wynne family.

In 1970, with bankruptcy looming, EC Osborne Ltd was bought by Tony and Judy Phillips and 'Cash and Carry Stationery Supermarket' selling was pioneered in the UK.

By 1980 the company comprised a chain of ten stationery supermarkets supported by a wholesale warehouse operation at Hockley in North Birmingham.

Ten years later the chain of shops had grown to 15 with the head office and central warehouse now relocated to Francis Road in Hay Mills, East Birmingham. The 20,000 sq. ft building also housed subsidiary companies PLG Distributors (wholesale stationery), Killeen and Bannister

(clearance stationery) and the Birmingham Boxfile Company (filing manufacturers).

Osbornes had acquired the small boxfile manufacturing company in 1983 when its annual turnover had been just £150,000. The 1990s were a decade of great change for most businesses and 'Osbornes' was no exception. Many new branches were opened; to facilitate that expansion in 1996 the file manufacturing business was disposed of: by then the file company which had once employed just five staff now employed 40 and had increased its turnover to £1.5 million.

In 1997 a complete re-imaging was undertaken with the company name being changed to Osborne Office Stationers and all the retail outlets refitted. Not that the name change was always noted by customers: as a result of the flashing neon signs in shop windows advertising photocopying at 5p, many clients would persist in referring to the firm as 'the 5p copy company'.

But whatever the name those pennies were adding up. By the dawn of the new millennium, with an annual turnover of £6 million, Osborne Office Stationers had posted 10 consecutive years of profit growth, with the number of retail outlets by now having risen to 24, and 150 staff employed. With Tony and Judy's son, Chris Phillips, now at the helm Osbornes' well deserved reputation, built up over many years for supplying quality stationery, office and art products at value for money prices, remains as valid today as it was in 1970 when the company passed into the ownership of the Phillips family.

Top left: Mr A Phillips, Chairman of Osborne Ltd, shows the Lord Mayor of Birmingham around their new warehouse during the Lord Mayor's visit to officially open the premises, March 1980. **Above Left:** *Owners of EC Osborne, Tony and Judy Phillips, 1972.*
Below left: An EC Osborne Stationery Superstore.
Below: One of Osborne's high street shops.

Charles E Cope & Sons (1919)

Copes Service Stations Ltd was formed in 1981 following the demerger of the family motor cycle business of Charles E Cope and Sons Ltd. Today it is entirely involved in owning and operating service stations situated throughout the West Midlands including Stourbridge, Tipton, Smethwick Handsworth, Halesowen and Kings Norton, with the firm's head office situated in Kidderminster.

The Copes story began back in 1919. In that year, former gunsmith Charles Cope, the grandfather of Copes Service Stations' present managing director Neville Cope, formed the firm of Charles E Cope & Sons. Back then the firm was a motor cycle retailer, based in an old bicycle shop. Charles looked after the shop whilst his sons, Frank and Arthur, took care of servicing and repairs.

After having served in the forces during the first world war the two boys believed there would be a growing market for motorcycles, and together with their father, they had bought the shop on the Hagley Road near Birmingham; the success of the business was very much dependent upon them being on the right side of the road.

To sell new motorcycles one had to be an agent - and each agent had an allocated area. Birmingham was already covered, but the Copes' Hagley Road premises were just outside the city boundary, which meant they could apply for dealerships.

In the immediate post World War I period, there were no petrol stations as we know them today; petrol was sold in two-gallon cans, on an exchange basis. The Copes stored their

Above: Founders, Frank (left) and Arthur Cope. Left: Charles Cope servicing a customer's motorcycle in 1920. Far left and below: Cope's Hagley Road branch in the 1920s.

fuel cans in an air raid shelter at the back of the shop, until they installed one of the country's first manual petrol pumps, at the beginning of 1920. This pump (Shell) now graces the hallway of their head office.

Arthur and his wife Irene, Neville's parents, lived over the shop and had the additional duty of operating the pump, and mixing petrol and benzene to customers' requirements. During the depression of the 1920s and 30s, their introduction of the new phenomenon, called hire purchase, or 'buying on the drip,' as it became known, helped their sales of motor cycles considerably. Copes financed the best HP deals themselves and used finance companies for the rest. For a deposit and regular monthly payments, many people bought new machines, which previously would have been beyond their means. Further depots were opened in Dudley in 1928 and Wolverhampton in 1931. The Dudley branch was managed by Percy Sturridge, Neville's godfather, who had started as the 'box boy', driving the box sidecar outfit which was used to collect or deliver machines. Percy later became a director,

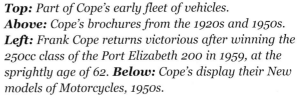

after returning to the company, following service in World War II, when he became a Colonel in the R.E.M.E.

In the late 1930s, with war clouds looming, Percy Sturridge had joined the Territorial Army as did many right minded chaps. With equal enthusiasm, the staff at Copes' Dudley Depot, decided to emulate their boss and follow him into the TA. When Arthur Cope visited the Dudley Depot, the day after World War II was declared, he found the place deserted except for one young lad - Arthur had to stay to run the show, for the rest of the war period.

The second world war was a lean period for the firm, which it survived, mainly by servicing machines for the armed forces. The government was, however, notoriously slow in paying, which caused Copes a few cash flow problems.

Following the end of the war however, motorcycle sales expanded. A motorcycle and sidecar was something many families aspired to. Copes' policy of financing many of its own hire purchase agreements, meant the firm

Top: *Part of Cope's early fleet of vehicles.*
Above: *Cope's brochures from the 1920s and 1950s.*
Left: *Frank Cope returns victorious after winning the 250cc class of the Port Elizabeth 200 in 1959, at the sprightly age of 62.* **Below:** *Cope's display their New models of Motorcycles, 1950s.*

always had recourse to repossessions, when payments were in default.

As a consequence, they always had useful stocks of second hand motorcycles and the end of the war found the firm with some very saleable machines. Stock levels were maintained by stipulating that no sale could be made, if no machine was offered in part exchange.

Arthur roamed far and wide in Europe buying up crates of war surplus machines at auction without really knowing what was in them. They bought thousands of BSA M20s, Matchless G3s, Ariel NH's and Norton 16H's and other makes which were no longer needed by the forces.

Copes prospered much from selling these EXWD machines and opened further branches, including Coventry in 1951, Birmingham in 1953, Newcastle, Staffs in 1954, Mansfield in

1957 and Worcester in 1961. They grew to become the second largest motor cycle dealers in Britain, eventually totalling 12 branches, selling some of those great names of the British motorcycle industry like Ariel, BSA, Royal Enfield, AJS, Norton, Triumph and Velocette. But small cars, such as the Mini were about to appear, and with the easing of Hire Purchase regulations, sales of cars began to overtake sales of motorcycles, the latter of which had totalled over 10,000 per annum in the late 1950's.

Arthur's son, Neville, returned from National Service in 1959, where he was commissioned in the RASC to work for the Hire Purchase company, Bowmakers, who had financed many of the Copes HP sales; and as a result of that experience, he joined the family firm, to manage the HP side of the business, in 1961.

During the 1960's, Douglas, Neville's elder brother, became managing director, with his cousin Roy. Douglas was to become president of the MAA in 1966, like his father, Arthur, 20 years before. They diversified the company into selling caravans, boats and finally petrol. Neville took over control of the petrol side of the business, in 1976.

One of the first steps Neville took, to build up petrol sales, was to be the first retail petrol company in the country to make their fuel prices visible from the road by erecting large signs, at each station, advertising their 4-star at 69.9p per gallon. These

Top: Cope's Hagley Road, showroom and headquarters in 1963. Above: The importance Cope's attached to service can be clearly seen in this photograph of part of their 1950s Repair Workshop.

signs were the forerunner of today's price pole signs.

In 1976 BP awarded Copes a 'Golden Nozzle' for selling 50,777 gallons of petrol in one week, at their Bearwood station, a national record for a four nozzle station, which still stands today. The triumph was achieved by filling up the tanks just prior to that year's autumn budget and then keeping prices at pre-budget levels for the next two weeks. The nozzle is now proudly displayed at their Head Office.

In 1981, the Cope family decided to each buy out a section of the family business. The Hagley Road garage, in Bearwood was sold to BP, to help finance the demerger. Neville Cope took on what had been the petrol sales division and began leasing further sites from BP. Eventually, Neville had taken on 12 sites, each of which had previously been closed, and which he then proceeded to 'build up'. The problem then, was that at each lease renewal, Neville was presented with a large rent increase. His answer was to buy petrol stations of his own and Neville

would eventually buy ten stations, all previously closed, which, of course, reduced the sale prices he had to pay.

Neville's rules for selecting a site were simple: first there had to be at least 1,000 vehicles an hour passing the site, or 750 on a dual carriageway; secondly it had to be on the 'going home' side of the road as most people buy fuel on their way home not on their way to work!

Neville Cope purchased these sites in the late 1980s during what Neville described as the 'mad period', when major oil companies would give large chunks of money towards buying and developing a site in order to get the supply contract. Today it is far harder to develop sites and Copes has just sold one site for residential development.

But the success of Copes Service Stations has not been simply in selling fuel: shop and valeting sales too are now a major part of business. Copes continues to evolve. Where once they had video libraries at all their sites, they are now considering bakeries and off licences, and have the National Lottery, cash machines, mobile phone cards and drop zones and other facilities at all their stations. In 2001, they are converting four of its station shops to Spar outlets, with three more to follow in 2002.

Life for the independent petrol retailers has never been easy, but with its long history, Copes know better than most how to cope with change.

Top and above left: *The new look Hagley Road garage in 1965, opened by Henry Cooper with Roy Cope looking on.* ***Below left:*** *Cope's Stourbridge Garage, now renamed Lance Cope, in memory of his son, Lance, who was killed in a motor accident in South Africa, in 1993.* ***Below right:*** *Neville Cope (left) with a Petrol Executive at the opening of their Dudley site.*

Number one for metals

So where do you go shopping for your sodium metasilcate? Today Asbury Brodie and Company, the metal and chemicals supplier is based at Number One, Dover Street Hockley.

The company was founded in 1932 by EW 'Bill' Asbury and Major JK 'Jack' Brodie, from whose surnames the company takes its name. The family nature of the firm over three generations is amply evidenced by the fact that Mrs Dorothy Jordan, the mother of the present chairman WG Jordan, had herself worked in the firm.

The company's famous Bull's Eye brand, an archery target with an arrow protruding from it, was first registered in 1933. Changed more than once, today the brand logo proudly displays the words 'ASBRO Metals and Chemicals'. In 1932 however, the business had begun at 55, George

Street, Birmingham, a location where the firm would stay for the next 29 years until the company moved to Hancock Road, Alum Rock in 1961.

With the descriptive telegraphic address of 'Chemalloy' the firm had soon became well known. The company set out to cover a wide field of industrial development including supplying a range of electrical resistance alloys and corrosion-resistant rustless irons and stainless steels.

*Above: Co-Founder, EW Asbury. **Right:** Co-Founder Major JK Brodie presenting the Queen with a brooch in 1957. **Below:** The company's Target Works premises in Hancock Road, Alum Rock, 1961.*

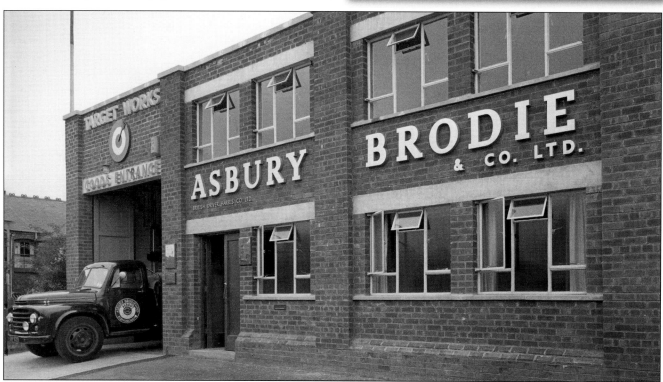

From the outset the firm dealt in nickel, nickel alloys, cobalt oxides, salts and stainless steel. Today the firm deals in zinc, copper-nickel anode materials as well as basic metal finishing chemicals, mainly concentrating on its own range of pre-treatment chemicals.

Even in its earliest days the firm offered a very wide range of products. Amongst its alloys for electric resistance for example the firm became agents for 'Nichrome' a registered trade name applied to a series of nickel-chromium alloys manufactured by the British Driver Harris company of Manchester. For working at temperatures of up to 900 degrees centigrade Nichrome was universally used for electric heating devices and Nichrome IV (a straight 80:20 nickel chromium) worked at much higher temperatures of up to 1150 degrees centigrade.

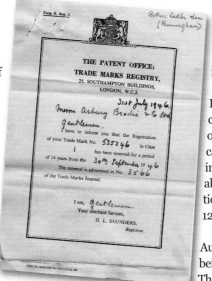

As a result of intensive research a super 80:20 nickel chromium was produced which was known as Nichrome V and which had double the life of other similar alloys. The alloy was used by many leading heating manufacturers for enclosed resistances of all types and for heating elements such as electric furnace resistances operated at extremely high temperatures for long periods.

A great deal of progress had been made in the manufacture of stainless steel in the 1940s and 50s. That progress was in large measure due to the insistent demand for corrosion and acid resistant materials for industrial applications and also improved methods of production. Very large quantities of stainless steel would be used for important chemical installations, for marine and mining equipment, automobiles, aircraft construction and for general decorative purposes. Such Austenitic Steels included the 18:8 and 12:12 chromium nickel steels which would resist corrosion in the presence of most acids and alkalis. The 12:12 grade was extremely ductile and was highly recommended for deep drawing and stamping operations, in many cases without intermediate annealing.

In contrast to stainless steel rustless iron is a chromium-iron alloy with a high percentage of chromium and a very small amount of carbon. The addition of chromium to iron increases its corrosion resistance and the absence of nickel reduces the cost of production. Straight chromium-iron contains between 12 and 30 percent of chromium.

Austenitic steels and rustless iron was soon being supplied as sheets, strip, rod and wire. The hot rolled, descaled sheets manufactured by the company, would have a surface almost equal to a cold rolled finish and after polishing would be free from defects. The company also had special facilities for supplying materials with a dull, bright or mirror polished finish and descaled polished sheets would be delivered in a perfectly flat condition.

Top: The 1961 opening ceremony of Asbury Brodie, Alum Rock. **Above:** *A Trade Mark Registry from the Patent Office, 1946.*

Like steel and iron pure nickel was manufactured in the form of sheet, strip, wire and also tape. It was used for electrical purposes mainly in connection with the manufacture of radio valves, sparking plug electrodes and other low electrical resistance devices. An interesting property of nickel is its comparatively low resistance as compared with the high resistance of many of its important alloys - and it has an electrical resistance some six times that of copper.

For non-electrical purposes large quantities of nickel were consumed in the form of nickel anodes and also for coinage, chemical apparatus and cooking and domestic utensils. The nickel supplied by the company was guaranteed to be of a 99/100 percent purity and could be produced in a hard bright temper, or in a bright fully annealed condition to suit customers requirements, free from superficial imperfections. In addition to the nickel alloys used for electrical purposes the company could also supply nickel-silver in a range of grades as well as a high grade copper-nickel alloy with a nickel content of around 45 percent.

One of the secrets of good electro-plating is the use of anodes which are produced from pure metals - commercially free from any impurities which will contaminate the bath and make clean working impossible. Only the purest metals were therefore good enough for Asbury Brodie. Nickel anodes could be supplied with a 99/100 percent purity:

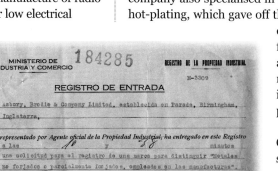

cast anodes which would deposit their nickel freely and evenly and wear away with a minimum of scrap. The company also specialised in heat-treated Rolled anodes for hot-plating, which gave off their nickel freely with a complete absence of sludge and free metallic particles - the anodes did not contain free nickel-oxide a source of danger if released even in minute particles.

Cadmium anodes too were supplied at 99/100 percent purity. This remarkable metal is an effective protection against rust and corrosion of iron and steel. It possesses the unique property of alloying with those base metals to form a perfect amalgam against corrosion. A cadmium deposit is highly tenacious and cadmium plated iron or steel articles remain rustless even after rough usage.

Copper anodes of 99/100 percent purity were supplied at a time when the use of copper was increasing for electro-deposition, not only for finished copper deposits but also as a base deposit on various metals for nickel and chromium plating.

Above: A Spanish Certificate of Registration, 1946.
Below left: A 1933 Trade Mark Acts Certificate of Registration. *Below:* Inside Target Works, 1961.

metal finishing industry encompassing the motor industry, the decorative industry, white goods, electronics and functional electroplating ; it also sells anode materials world wide. Everyone in metal finishing from jobbing platers to Rolls Royce motor cars uses products from Asbury Brodie's technically competent products of high quality, which are backed up by an unrivalled service.

A bewildering array of products are now supplied and stocked by the company. Not only does the firm manufacture pre-treatment, chromating and phosphating processes, it sells more than 70 chemical products ranging from activated carbon to zinc oxide and more than half a dozen anode materials including: nickel, copper, brass, zinc, tin and chrome.

In association with INCO Ltd, the world's leading producer of nickel, based in Canada, Asbury Brodie also supplies a wide range of nickel based products.

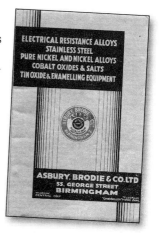

It was however not just metals which were being sold: cobalt oxides were being supplied in quantity under the Bull's Eye Brand. Black oxide of cobalt is used as a body stain to neutralise the iron which is present in the clay used in the making of pottery. Cobalt oxide is used as a glaze stain and for that purpose it is essential that the oxide should be up to strength and of unvarying quality and texture in order to produce the beautiful and rich blue colours for which famous pottery manufacturers had gained a world wide reputation. Cobalt oxide would also be used extensively in the vitreous enamelling industry. An alternative to cobalt oxide is cobalt chloride, whilst cobalt slats: cobalt sulphate, cobalt acetate and cobalt hydrate were used as driers in the manufacture of paints.

All of these activities are carried out from the company's factory and offices in Dover Street Hockley

The ASBRO company manages to hit the commercial bull's eye every time!

Above left: Mr GA Jordan outside Alum Rock Works, 1969. Above right: An Asbury Brodie Booklet. Below: Asbury Brodie's factory and offices in Hockley.

Finally nickel chromium alloy was manufactured in the form of enamel racks, perret bars and points and knife edge fusing bars. This alloy was specially designed for use at the high temperatures required by the vitreous enamel industry. The alloy could be worked continuously at temperatures up to 1100 degrees Centigrade without warping, scaling or cracking, and the life of the material under normal working conditions would be many times greater than mild steel or cast iron.

Today the company's main markets in the UK are the

A lesson in charity

F ircroft College of Adult Education was founded by George Cadbury in 1909 as an educational charity to provide higher and general education opportunities in a residential environment.

Initially only for men, since 1980 the College has also included women on all its courses. The College is situated in a large early 20th century family residence 'Primrose Hill', George Cadbury's own home, set in 6 acres of gardens and grounds in Bristol Road, Selly Oak.

The college began its life however based at The Dell in Oak Tree Lane where it remained until 1957. For its first five years Fircroft flourished. Correspondence courses were started and even summer schools for women were held in 1910.

George Cadbury's vision was to provide an education which was generally broadening, not simply the means by which men might educate themselves to do better jobs; he envisaged mature men aged 25 to 35 coming to study groups of subjects such as economics, history, art and drama. But whatever the subject they would gain something more important, namely the art of living together in a group of 40 to 50 students which he believed developed the character and enlarged the mind.

During the first world war The Dell was taken over as a hospital and the staff who remained were transferred to Holland House, Woodbrooke.

Between the wars Fircroft again flourished and expanded. It was recognised by the Department of Education in 1925 but still remained wholly dependent upon George Cadbury until his death.

Left: Founder, George Cadbury. *Below:* Staff and students of 1920-1921. *Bottom:* The original Fircroft College in Oak Tree Lane.

and support needs as well as underdeveloped interpersonal and group skills. Many also come from disadvantaged social or economic backgrounds.

In 1939 war closed Fircroft for a second time and the Dell was turned into a remand home. Fircroft re-opened in Oak Tree Lane in 1947 by which time temporary buildings were already in use at Primrose Hill.

After George Cadbury's death in 1954 Fircroft had to become self supporting. Cadbury's son, Christopher, became chairman of the Trust and Governors. In 1957 Christopher Cadbury moved the college to the Cadbury family home, Primrose Hill, the house where he had been born.

Fircroft would justify George Cadbury's convictions and effort by providing thousands of young adults with the opportunity they would never otherwise have had; the chance to take time off from the driving necessity of earning a living in order to consider the purpose of life. It enriched their minds and their personalities; and through them Fircroft's humanitarian and liberal influences would extend into countless other lives.

Inevitably many students whose horizons were extended and whose academic talent were nurtured eventually left their previous occupations to take on more demanding work, as ministers of religion, social workers, trade union officials, politicians, lawyers and managers. One of the first students became Birmingham's first probation officer, another became Lord Mayor and others were elected Members of Parliament. Many more however returned to their jobs and helped raise the standards of their colleagues, in accordance with the aims of the founder. Throughout its existence the College's mission has been to promote social justice by providing adults with an excellent learning environment for personal and professional development.

The College now has a long history of enabling adult learners to have a second chance of education, many of whom have had a number of unsuccessful and alienating learning experiences during and after leaving school. Students come with a wide range of learning

In the final year of the 20th century, of the 779 students, 72 percent would be female, 41 percent from ethnic minorities, 5 percent suffered a disability, 91 percent were over the age of 25 and 54 percent were unemployed or without a source of income.

Today the College offers a range of programmes for its students. 'Fircroft Studies' is a one year full-time access course with key skills at its centre, plus units on humanities, social sciences, mathematics, science and information technology: Achieving a nationally recognised Access Certificate will gain students entry to university. There is also a programme of weekday and weekend residential Short Courses including 'return to study', African-Caribbean history and IT. Community-based projects and courses are also based at the College and off-site in the inner city with residential elements an integral part of them.

Above left: *An aerial view of Fircroft College, 1959.*
Above right: *Private Study in the George Cadbury Library, 1950s.* ***Below:*** *The College's first Award Ceremony, December 1998.*

Dockers to PPG - a polished performance

The original Docker Brothers company, the forerunner of the present PPG Ladywood business, which has made such a great contribution to the local economy, began its life in 1881.

It all started with the enterprise of brothers, Dudley and William Docker - they were joined by a third brother, Ludford, in 1886. The three brothers were already known in the area for their sporting and athletic prowess, and were extremely well known in the Midlands, and indeed throughout the country, as sound and forceful cricketers. Ludford especially – playing for Shrewsbury's Eleven, in 1887, in what was virtually the first Test Match in Australia.

As is often the case with large and successful businesses, the beginning was a humble one in 1881. Docker Brothers, as the business was known, was housed in two Birmingham railway arches under the Great Western Railway at Allcock Street, Deritend. According to the balance sheet for December of that year, the capital was £1,800; the stock valued at £654 and the plant at £225.

At this time the only material sold was Stoving Black Varnish, and they did not even make this. It was bought from a manufacturer in the Black Country in 40-gallon barrels, and was then put into 1-gallon cans and re-delivered to Dockers' customers who were chiefly makers of hollow-ware, bicycles, bedsteads and umbrellas. With the phenomenal growth of these industries in Birmingham, it is not surprising that the demand for Stoving Black exceeded supply.

It is recorded that there were occasions when Mr Dudley Docker used to persuade the carter who had delivered the barrels, to re-deliver the small cans to Dockers' customers. When this manoeuvre could not be arranged, the cans were delivered by an employee Mr Herbert Preston who made the rounds by horse and cart.

Above: Dudley and Ludford Docker.
Below: First works outing, 1923.

Docker Brothers rapidly established a market for its varnish and five years later, when Ludford Docker came into the business, the capital had risen to about £8,000 and the stock to £1,250. Although sales had increased steadily, the business still consisted largely of Stoving Black, but instead of simply factoring, the company began making its own varnish. A family of the name of Stack, father and two sons, were engaged in making varnish under the supervision of a Mr Hunt, who joined the company as a varnish consultant from Tabor Trego.

The business had now grown so much that the Allcock Street premises had become quite inadequate, and in 1886 a small freehold paint-making factory, costing just under £2,000, with white lead grinding mills and colour-making plant already installed, was purchased in Rotton Park Street, Ladywood from Badams Brothers, a paint manufacturing business. These first premises were located on land adjacent to the present company site – which in later years became a car park.

Larger premises meant that Docker Brothers were now in a position to manufacture a wider range of products, but were still unable to make enough varnish to meet demand and a quantity was purchased in barrels from makers in Derby and Merton in Surrey.

The workforce consisted of Mr Bone, Works Manager, nine men making varnish, four making paint, plus Herbert Preston and his horse and cart – a kind of salesman!

The raw materials on which the early varnishes were based came from far and wide. They were what is known as fossil resin gums. Of these, the Kauri and Sierra Leone Copal were the most frequently used in the manufacture of fine varnishes. Kauri gum was found in New Zealand. Its source was trees which had become extinct (hence 'fossil') and were lying a few feet below the surface of the ground.

Docker Brothers were always on the look-out for new markets and by 1901 they were winning large contracts for the export market. This was in addition to the home markets which by now had extended to railways, and to a

*Above: A highly ornate varnish label, 1898. **Below:** Docker Brothers works outing to Henley-on-Thames, 1930.*

lesser extent, shipping companies. Dudley Docker had become a Director of the Metropolitan Carriage and Wagon Company at Saltley and in 1902 he brought about the amalgamation of eight or nine carriage and wagon companies and formed what was known as the Metropolitan Amalgamated Carriage & Wagon Company. In 1904 Docker Brothers was absorbed into this combine but still traded under its original name. The Head Office was situated at Metropolitan Works and production remained at Rotton Park Street Works.

During 1904 more land adjoining the original freehold land in Rotton Park Street, was leased from the Birmingham Canal Navigation Company, making the total area of the Works about one and a quarter acres.

In 1913 an option was obtained on the land where the present factory stands, and a garage, gum store, two varnish-making shops and two bays for tank storage of varnish were built.

The First World War saw Docker Brothers busily engaged in supplying paint for munitions, transport and shell varnishes. After the war the business continued to flourish and more people joined the company. Things were very

different in those days. Wages were comparatively low and hours were long and there were no comforts in the way of mess-rooms. The staff had no dining-room, but a few senior executives lunched in state at their roll-top desks from trays brought up by the caretaker's wife.

The Siberia Mill, the first paint manufacturing shop, was built in 1919. The mill derives its name from a remark made by Mr Charles Lewis, a former Works Manager, who for some time had worked in Russia. One day on visiting the Mill, which is furthest from the main building and at the time was very cold, he exclaimed; "Blimey, its like being in Siberia" – and after all he should know!

Vickers Ltd purchased in 1921 a controlling interest in the Metropolitan Company, and in 1927 Pinchin Johnson & Co Ltd bought the Docker Brothers business which became part of what was then one of the largest paint manufacturing groups in the world. It was not till 1928 that the old Works in Rotton Park Street was finally closed.
The Second World War found Dockers again supplying

Top: Siberia Mill paint making shop, 1923.
Above: A photograph of the Sales Team, 1948.

paint for munitions, camouflage and transport, as well as aircraft dopes and finishes. The staff was depleted considerably but the switch from peace-time production to war-time essentials was made smoothly and effectively. Even in July 1942 when most of the Rotton Park Street factory lay in smoking ruins, after an enemy air raid, there was only a momentary pause in the steady flow of materials. Tangled machinery was replaced, temporary buildings were erected and sister firms lent a helping hand. The office staff "made do" in cramped quarters in various parts of the city, and the work went on.

On Friday 2nd July 1948, the new Lewis Mill paint shop, built to replace the building destroyed at Docker Brothers during the war, was formally opened. The new building had been named as a tribute to the Works Director, Mr Charles Lewis, who had given a lifetime of service to the company and had been the driving force behind the difficult work of reconstruction. Hundreds of gallons of spilt varnish had presented the most difficult problem in the factory rebuilding. A bronze plaque commemorating Mr Lewis's achievement was unveiled during the opening ceremony.

As the company entered the 1950s, it experienced a time of rapid expansion. The boundaries of the factory now extended to the far end of Rotton Park Street. The company directors were keen to exploit the new mood of optimism which prevailed in the commercial world after the end of the war and they decided to launch an advertising campaign greater than any the company had previously undertaken. It is recorded that in 1952 the advertising budget was dramatically increased to

£15,500, to cover catalogues, exhibitions, giveaways and advertisements in some thirty trade journals.

No one was surprised when the result of the campaign was an increase in demand and although Synthetic Resins had been manufactured since the 1930s, plans to double the production capacity were drawn up and £30,000 worth of new equipment was purchased for the task.

Expansion continued into the 1960s. Pinchin Johnson, the parent company, moved its Birmingham Depot from premises in King Edwards Place to Rotton Park Street,

*Top right: Rotton Park Street factory after a 1942 enemy air raid. **Above:** 1948, the unveiling of a memorial plaque in honour of four firefighters whose lives were lost during the Blitz in June 1942. **Left:** Ladywood Old Colleagues Association Annual Reunion, 1959 - Mr Cyril Hastilow, President (left) with Mr Leonard Barker. (2001 saw the 50th Annual Reunion of the L.O.C.A. Company employees were, and still are, eligible for membership of this exclusive association, upon completion of 25 years of unbroken service.*

into a building adjacent to Docker Brothers. PJ's production facility in West Heath was also relocated to the Docker Brothers premises and to absorb this, a new paint shop was created out of a former storage area, subsequently called the Westminster Mill. This produced general industrial finishes and large consignments were supplied to the steel furniture industry, a new and rapidly growing market. Apart from the opening of Westminster Mill, production was also increased in the Siberia Mill, Lewis Mill and in the Ready Mixing Department.

The company experienced another change in its ownership. Courtaulds, the giant textile concern, acquired Pinchin Johnson Paints in

1960 and a worldwide marine-coatings business, International Paint in 1968. (In April 1972, Pinchin Johnson changed its trading name to International Pinchin Johnson and by the early 1980s the whole paint division became known as International Paint, although the Rotton Park Street business continued to restrict its activities to original vehicle finishes, refinish

paints, industrial and aviation products.)

The 1960s also saw the arrival of a new technology in the paint industry – it was called Electropaint. In this process, an item to be painted is immersed in a bath of electropaint and a current is passed through it. The paint then attaches itself in an even film and the most recessed areas are coated. As early as 1961, the first electropaint was developed for petrol tanks.

1968 saw yet further expansion in synthetic resin manufacture when probably the largest induction heated resin reactor in Britain, nicknamed "Jumbo" was installed. It weighed sixteen tons, was fourteen feet in height and was specially designed for high temperature reaction. The reactor could make practically all known types of resin. The plant which cost £120,000, produced resin in batches of 2,500 gallons to 5,000 gallons. To make one batch, it consumed the amount of electricity used by the average householder in two years.

In the late 1970s, cathodic resin technology enabled higher quality finishes to be produced. The success of

*Top right: Poster for the Docker Brothers Dramatics Society, 1952. **Left:** 'Jumbo' Resin Reactor, 1968. **Below left:** Valley Mill, 1965 - designed especially for the production of car refinishing paints. **Below:** A Flowline advertisement for the 1973 British Grand Prix.*

From Docker Brothers to PPG
100 YEARS OF CRICKET

responded. At that time they were able to supply a range of over 3,500 colours.

the process led to the company investing £1 million in a new Cathodic Clear Resin Plant. The market continued to grow for this product and it was expanded in 1989. Cathodic electropaint is the method now used for priming in most car plants and many other manufacturing facilities throughout the world. This was also the time when there was a high demand for refinish paint products and the company

In 1982 the £300,000 technologically advanced refinish plant for the manufacture of 'Acryline' was completed. Acryline was the first of the second generation of 2-pack acrylics, the nearest yet that a repair material had come to equalling the performance of the original car finish.

December 1980 saw the closure of the former Cellon Aviation Paint Plant in Kingston-on-Thames. The aviation production was moved to a newly opened mill at Rotton Park Street named "Kingston". New offices and laboratories were also created to establish the new business at Ladywood.

In 1985, the Rotton Park Street business was acquired by PPG Industries Inc. - an American coatings, glass, fibre glass and chemicals group. PPG Industries was founded in 1883 as the Pittsburgh Plate Glass Company. They acquired a brush firm Patton Paint Company and an auto paint company in 1900, which became the foundation of PPG's Coatings and Resins business.

Since that time the company has continued to adapt and respond to changes in the market and has sought to be at the forefront of the industry, producing the types of finishes demanded by modern manufacturing. The business is now very different from the one run by the three Docker Brothers at the close of the nineteenth century.

Top left: PPG's participation in the 1985 Birmingham Lord Mayor's procession - 'The International Year of Youth' was the procession theme and PPG's cricket float celebrated one hundred years of the 'Docker Shield'. The Docker Shield is believed to be the oldest school-boy cricket competition in the world, so during the procession they quite naturally played cricket - on the back of a lorry. Above: A PPG tanker outside the Ladywood factory. Left: PPG's headquarters at PPG Place, Pittsburgh, Pa, USA.

Big train sets

Alstom Transport Ltd is still a relatively new name for Birmingham folk. The UK home of this huge international company based in France, is in Leigh Road, Washwood Heath. But although the name may seem quite new the corporate ancestors of the firm have had associations with Birmingham going back to the reign of Queen Victoria.

The founder of the Alstom's earliest UK ancestor, the 'Metropolitan' company, was Joseph Wright a London coach builder who owned most of the stagecoaches running between London and Birmingham.

Wright established himself at Saltley Birmingham, and ever since then railway carriages and wagons have been built in the city by his successors.

Joseph Wright died in 1859 and his son took over the company. By 1870 the firm had begun manufacturing tramcars. By 1912 the company was producing its famous 'Metropolitan' carriage.

Above left: *Founder, Joseph Wright.*
Right: *A 1932 metal bodied bus, designed by Metropolitan - Cammell Carriage & Wagon Company Ltd.* **Below:** *An Orient Express Sleeping Car built by Metro - Cammell.*

During the first world war the firm became involved with building tanks . That led indirectly in 1919 to the company being acquired by Vickers.

Vickers and the Cammell Laird company merged in 1929 to form Metropolitan Cammell . In 1932 the company began to produce double decker buses. The design for the all-metal bus bodies was initially developed, by what was by then known as the Metropolitan-Cammell Carriage & Wagon Company Ltd, with a view to mass producing them.

Making buses was not to last long. 1939-45 found the firm once more producing tanks; the company would produce 80 percent of all tanks used by our forces - even though the majority of workers were also involved in Home Guard duties. Following the outbreak of peace however

production would return to public transport and by 1952 the company was providing coaches for the London Underground, a contract which would see the company supply 80 percent of all rolling stock running on the Underground network. In fact the company had supplied carriages to the Underground as early as 1902, but by the early 1960s the firm had supplied over 2,500 coaches to the London Underground and introduced the famous unpainted aluminium alloy exteriors which replaced the earlier steel bodies.

At the same time the company had been supplying diesel railcars and in 1955 had become the first private firm to produce such units for British Railways. Inspired by such work the company became involved in the Blue Pullman in 1960; these high speed luxury Pullmans were diesel units purpose-built to run on the Midland line between Wolverhampton and London and continued in production through the 1960s and the 1970s.

The Metropolitan firm became wholly part of the Laird Group when Vickers sold its half of the company back to Lairds in 1970. In 1965, almost in anticipation, the group had already shortened its name to Metropolitan Cammell Ltd - better known in the early days as Met Cam.

In 1975 the company began producing KCRC but, despite having enjoyed sales from all corners of the globe the future was beginning to look a little bleak.

Even so the late 1970s would see the company producing units for the Kowloon Cantonese Railway with all its Mass Transit Rolling Stock - a contract which would later lead to orders for a major refurbishment of stock in the 1990s.

By the mid 1980s however a gap had appeared in the order book. The work force was scaled down to a skeleton staff of just 50. The company changed its manufacturing strategy to become an assembler of rolling stick.

By 1987 the company was producing the 156 DMU Super Sprinter the forerunners of the modern Multiple Unit and supplied 228 vehicles. In 1989 Metropolitan Cammell was bought by GEC Alsthom.

Throughout the 1990s the company was involved in Eurostar, the 465 EMU, Nightstock, Northern Line, the Jubilee Line and the Arlanda airport link in Sweden before being floated on the stock exchange in 1998 - under the new name of Alstom.

By the opening years of the 21st century Alstom was making DMUs (Diesel Multiple Units), EMUs (Electric Multiple Units) and the High Speed tilting train, stock which could be seen all over the United Kingdom - the Gatwick Express, South West trains, Scotrail First North Western and First Great Western - all a long way from horse drawn coaches!

Above left: A tank produced during the second world war. Above: The Blue Pullman, built by Metro - Cammell, and started service in 1960. Below: The Juniper Class 460 Gatwick Express.

Kappa SSK - from the beginning

Smith, Stone and Knight was founded in Landor Street, Birmingham in 1862. An excise duty that had been levied on the 'luxury' item of paper had recently been cancelled, creating a demand for newly afford-able papers in the UK and in the burgeoning markets of the Empire. Surpris-ingly of the three founders, Thomas Bird Smith, John Benjamin Stone and Frederick Knight, only Thomas Smith knew anything about the paper making trade. He had previously worked with his uncle, paper maker James Baldwin of Kings Norton.

The partnership worked very well and the business found its niche in the market. In 1873 the company purchased a site in Cranemore Street, Nechells (more often known as Grove Mill or Birmingham Paper Mills) and incorporated more paper machines. Around this time, the reputation of the firm began to grow. SSK became famous for its 'Grove Brown' and the product ranges were extended. A bag factory turning out 100 tonnes of paper bags was later added.

Over the years, the range of SSK products increased to include such diverse items as blue sugar bags, wadding for bullet cartridges, blackout curtains, concrete slab paper, pastels and special paper for sound insulation in cars such as the mini and the Morris Minor.

The company was expanded even further by its procure-ment of the Aston Manor Paper Mills in 1899 and the Avonside Mills in Bristol in 1908. Always at the forefront of technology, tests were carried out in 1906 on a new steam engine for the Aston Mill. Eighty years on, in 1985, the company started up a combined heat and power plant run by a gas turbine.

Above: TB Smith, Sir JB Stone and F Knight, founders of Smith Stone & Knight. Below: Recycling in the 1890s - Rag Picking.

The enterprise became a limited company in 1894. Messrs Smith, Stone and Knight were still at the helm and the partnership flourished until the death of Thomas Smith in 1905. It was soon after that Sir JB Stone and Mr Knight retired from any active part in the director-ship of the company.

1909 was a bumper year. Production in the Landor Street Mills was 120 tonnes of sugar paper per week while at the Grove Mill 100 tons of bag papers and assorted products were produced each week.

A family tradition developed at the business with sons of two of the founding fathers becoming involved in the firm. T P Smith became chairman of the company and his brother P S Smith was responsible for the running of the Bristol Mill. B W Stone directed the Aston Mills and

O H Stone directed the Grove Mill. The family tradition extended to a third generation with brothers E S Smith, P S Smith and N S Smith, a family connection which endured right into the 1970s. One story of the Smith dynasty tells of a Saturday morning when an elderly and somewhat scruffy member of the clan was looking around the Mill at Aston. From his window, seeing what he believed to be a tramp, the mill manager challenged the elderly 'intruder', who turned out to be his boss!

The firm made steady progress until the first world war which caused problems for the company, as eager young

Top: The Bag Making Room. **Left:** *An early SSK paper machine.* **Below:** *Sheet cutting.*

men signed up for the army. During this time many of SSK's staff distinguished themselves on the field of valour including a former apprentice at the Grove Mill.

Between the wars 1918 - 1939
A combination of bad luck and financial difficulties caused by the war made for a rough time in the 1920s.

After the war, the company made provision for the returning soldiers, '...Not only to provide employment for the whole of their staff and works people who had been fighting, but to provide a fund for the assistance of those who had been disabled or incapacitated from doing the work they were engaged in before the war.' However, measures for recovery were successful and SSK emerged from the 'Depression' a leaner, fitter organisation, having in the meantime acquired Andre Poll and Co, based in Ghent.

Sir John Benjamin Stone MP - Photographer and paper maker

Nestling in the vaults of the Birmingham Central Reference Library, is a unique photographic legacy belonging to the people of Birmingham. It is the life work of one man, Benjamin Stone. It comprises 22,000 mounted prints, 2,500 glass lantern slides, 600 stereo-scopic prints and many personal scrapbooks, journals and papers. Stone was the epitome of the Victorian entrepreneur, adventurer and innovator and a pioneer of new techniques of printing and plate developing.

Left: Supervising the Salle. Below: SSK's early administration team.

Ever the innovator, Stone was one of the earliest exponents of the dry plate process, which meant that the old and inconvenient method of having to develop plates on the spot was made obsolete. He also pioneered the no-fade platinum printing process which means that his prints are with us today.

Benjamin Stone was born in Aston near Birmingham in 1838 and was immersed in the world of business upon leaving school. He entered local politics in the 1860s becoming Sutton Coldfield's first Mayor in 1886. He was knighted in 1892 and became MP for East Birmingham in 1895, a seat he held until his retirement in 1910.

King Edward VII asked Sir Benjamin to photograph his Coronation in 1902. However, this was not technically feasible given the standard of photographic chemicals at the time.

The second world war 1939 - 1945

More trying times were ahead with the arrival of another war in 1939. The 1940s saw a steady destruction of the company buildings by one air raid after another. 1944 brought a bitter dispute with the Board of Trade over the compulsory requisition of part of the company's bag factory in Crown Street, (this factory had given its name to the company's world renowned Crown Blue paper).

However the Dunkirk spirit won through and the cessation of hostilities brought a massive increase in the demand for paper, which brought a much needed boost to sales. The firm became a public company in 1948. Astonishingly the firm was still making deliveries using horse and cart at this time.

*Top: Delivering by horse and cart. **Above left:** Smith Stone & Knight's Certificate of Incorporation from 1905. **Right:** Bag Makers.*

Rebuilding the company

The 1950s were a time of expansion and a new mill at Cranemore Street was built where paper making was then concentrated.

During the 1960s manufacturing carried on in Bristol and at the subsidiary in Manchester. This centred mainly on box making.

By the early 1970s, SSK had been bought by the Dolan Packaging Group which in turn was bought by the Swedish nationalised wood products company, ASSI.

In October 1976 a works consortium won the grand total of £29,000 on Vernon Pools. Management feared an immediate walkout, but the sudden fortune didn't turn anyone's head and no one left to retire on his winnings.

Building for the future 1980 - 2000

The mill survived through the recession in the early 1980s, a time when British paper machines were closing almost weekly. Discussions started which lead to increasing the mill's capacity with the addition of another paper machine. In the meantime new technology had arrived with computer control systems.

After acquisition by the Dutch Company KNP BT in 1987, a project began at SSK, to build a new high-tech paper

Below: An aerial view of Kappa SSK.

machine, which, by the end 1989 was in full operation.

In 1998 KNP BT sold their packaging division, of which SSK was a part, to a joint finance house put together by Cinven Ltd and CVC Capital Partners BV.

The existing KNP BT Packaging management continued to run the company under the new name Kappa Packaging. As a result Smith Stone and Knight changed its name for the first time in its history to Kappa SSK.

By 2000 Kappa SSK had increased capacity to 180,000 tonnes of recycled paper, offering a dedicated service to the corrugating industry. The new century brought its developments and in 2000 a fully automated Robotic Warehouse was installed. The company maintains accreditation to the recognised quality standards ISO 9001 and ISO 14001.

Following the acquisition of the French corrugating company SCAO and AssiDoman, Kappa Packaging became one of Europe's leading paper based packaging companies with paper and board capacity of approximately 3.1 million tonnes. The company comprises of 114 production sites spread over 16 European countries with 17,000 employees and a network of additional sales offices.

High levels of investment continue throughout the group as Kappa aims to be a dominating factor in the packaging market into the future.

An integral partner for Kappa SSK is Kappa Paper Recycling which is responsible for supplying the recovered paper, which is the main raw material for SSK's process. This recovered paper is made up of old cardboard boxes sourced mainly from industrial and retail outlets and mixed papers sourced mainly from domestic collection.

Kappa Paper Recycling (KPR) was originally established in 1913 by Smith Stone & Knight under the name of the Birmingham Waste Company and quickly established depots for the collection of recovered paper across the Midlands. Difficult times in the 1920s saw closure of depots that had been opened in the first world war with only Birmingham and Bristol depots remaining operational. The start of the second world war led to an increase in recycling activity and depots were opened in Nottingham, Sheffield and Cheltenham. The Birmingham, Cheltenham and Sheffield depots were bombed and it was 1942 before the Birmingham and Cheltenham depots were operational again.

Following the war the Company continued to expand its activities and

by 1971 it had 11 depots. As ownership of Smith Stone & Knight changed and the requirement for additional material grew the less economic depots were closed and activities concentrated in key areas and by 1985 there were only four depots.

Strong international and local demand for recovered papers led to increased competition and pressure on the costs of collection which resulted in the closure of two more depots leaving only the current Birmingham and Nottingham depots which together supply 100,000 tonnes of paper to Kappa SSK almost 50 per cent of its annual requirement.

This tonnage is collected local to the depots from industrial and commercial sites and from domestic sources using paper banks and household collection.

The Birmingham Depot has had a number of homes from its original base in Moland Street to Belmont Row then Bordersley Green and finally to its current location in Saltley.

Above: A lorry unloading tonnes of paper to be recycled.
Below: Emptying one of the 600 igloos located around the Midlands area.

From farthings to euros

Are there any numismatists out there? Coin collectors that is. How many of us picked up a good part of our history lessons simply from looking at the coins in our pockets. Before decimalisation came along we could grab a fistful of pennies and see the faded face of Queen Victoria, her son Edward VII, and the two Georges as well as our own dear Queen Elizabeth. Kids today only get to see our current monarch, and more than half of them would have difficulty telling you who her father was. Not so for us.

Hanging around under a gas lamp looking at pennies closely one sometimes saw a tiny letter H tucked beneath Britannia's shield. Why was that there for, what did it mean? The answer supplied by the older brother who knew his pocket money was that it meant that the coin had come from the Birmingham Mint. And an even smarter boy might just know that the H stood for Heaton, the surname of the Mint's founder.

The business was founded by Ralph Heaton II. After finishing an apprenticeship with Thomas Willetts as a die sinker Ralph went to work with his father, Ralph Heaton the first who had set up his business in 1794. The first Ralph Heaton had commenced his business as a brass founder in Shadwell Street in 1794 and had five sons, John, William, George, Reuben and Ralph, who all eventually joined the firm.

After completing his apprenticeship ,which he had begun in 1810, the young Ralph set up his own business in a corner of his father's workshop. At the end of 1817 Ralph's father conveyed to him by deed, land at Icknield Street and extending towards Shadwell Street containing a tenement and a shop. It was at this site that Ralph set up the business which would eventually become The Birmingham Mint.

Top left: Founder Ralph Heaton II.
Above: A coin struck by Ralph Heaton & Sons in 1872.
Below: The Mint at Icknield Street, 1862.

the present day. The first development was the making of blanks for coinage and in 1853 a contract was made with the Royal Mint for 500 tons of copper coinage consisting of pennies, half pennies, farthings, half farthings and quarter farthings.

This coincided with a time when the British government had decided to re-fashion the whole of the copper coinage and introduce bronze coinage (which itself in time would be replaced by copper plated steel, the material in use today). The change placed great pressure on the Royal Mint and it was a stroke of good fortune that The Mint in Birmingham was already established as a going concern.

The work in the earliest days was highly varied but included brass founding, stamping, piercing and expanding to light fittings. Patents were taken out by Ralph I for a button shank machine, machines for drilling and ornamenting buttons, for cutting out biscuits for the Royal Navy, for rifling gun barrels and the design of steam engines. Later the brass foundry side of the business was developed and articles such as candle snuffers, cloak buckles, prison bowls and chandeliers for the new gas industry were made.

A one man band at the outset, Ralph was joined in the business by two of his sons, including Ralph Heaton III with the firm's name changing over time from Heaton & Son to Heaton & Sons in recognition of that change.

Coining started in 1850 with the purchase at auction of the necessary equipment from the Boulton Watt Soho Mint. At around the same time a technical consultancy business was begun which continues to

For some 44 years after its founding the firm had remained at its original premises in Bath Street but the coining business had meant expansion.

In 1860 the present Icknield Street site, then around an acre, was bought and the company moved in 1862. Some 300 people would be being employed there. Over the years the business would expand down Icknield Street and up to the corner of Warstone Lane.

A breakdown of its ancient machinery shut down the Royal Mint for five months in 1876 resulting in a major increase in work for the Birmingham Mint: in that year it produced more than a million bronze farthings, almost seven million halfpennies and a staggering eleven million pennies.

The firm not only made coins but also sold complete mints,

*Top left: The original coin press room, 1862. **Above left:** The strip rolling mill 1862. **Left:** A furnace for producing slab and bar ingots, circa 1960.*

particularly in the Far east. In 1887 it got the contract to build and equip the Canton Mint. The entire equipment of the Imperial Mint at Canton in China included no fewer than 90 coining presses and was completed in 18 months - following negotiations which had been going on for more than 20 years.

The business became a limited liability company in 1889 and as part of the new arrangements Ralph Heaton IV was to be employed as General Manager, with his brothers Gerald Heaton as Works Manager and Walter Heaton as Company Secretary.

By that time coinage was the chief product and contracts for coinage not only included supplying the British government but eventually over 100 other governments and issuing authorities across the world including: Canada, Chile, Italy, Denmark, Germany, Hong Kong and Borneo.

In 1911 the firm lost its monopoly to supply the Royal Mint with coinage and began sharing the contract with the Kings Norton Metal Company, the producers of a commemorative Millennium medal in 1901. The full implications of sharing that contract would bear unexpected fruit many decades later.

But for the moment war was the major question. The 1914-18 world war led to labour shortages and a commercial concern about customer base and raw materials.

In 1918 at the end of the Great War the Kings Norton Metal Company became part of Nobel Industries. The following year saw the last issue of coins with Heaton 'H' mark from the Birmingham Mint.

Meanwhile Nobel Industries merged in 1926 to become ICI metals division and in the 1930s it moved to Witton and became the Kynoch Mint.

The second world war presented a particular problem, as at its end, the Birmingham Mint was left with run down machinery that badly needed maintenance due to it having worked a 6 1/2 day week for the whole of the war.

Surprisingly in the previous quarter of a century the production of coins had amounted to not more than 10-20 percent of business each year. Since the end of the first world war main production in terms of tonnage had been rolled metals - mainly copper and brass. This was followed by the production of copper tubing as well as fittings for water pipes, engraved nameplates, washers for the motor industry and pressings for the electrical industry.

Above: A late 19th century view of The Birmingham Mint. Left: Staff weighing and bagging coins circa 1960. Below: The mayor's visit, 1947.

The Heaton family connection was maintained until 1962 when Ralph Heaton V retired as Company Secretary. That year saw ICI's Kynoch Mint become part of a newly formed IMI company which would soon join a consortium made up of the Royal Mint, Birmingham Mint and Kynoch Mint.

Between 1967 and 1975 the Minting operation of the Birmingham Mint was carried out in premises in Warstone Lane; it was eventually moved back to The Mint site when the tube and water fittings side of the business was sold off.

In 1988 the Birmingham Mint Group plc bought the Green Duck Corporation in the USA but problems lay ahead. After poor results in 1990 IMI plc, of which Kynoch Mint was a part, obtained the controlling interest in the Birmingham Mint in January 1991 and moved the IMI minting operation onto the Birmingham Mint site. The minting division was then renamed as The IMI Birmingham

Mint. A Nickel Plating line for nickel-plated coin blanks and coins was commissioned. More acquisitions were planned and in 1993 Casino Tokens inc. of the USA was bought.

The company name reverted to The Birmingham Mint in 1998 when there was a management buy-out supported by the '3i' investment bank. Consolidation and rationalisation followed and in 1999, the American companies were closed down.

In August 2001, the company was acquired by a former Chief Executive, Roland Veron. The company is continuing to trade as The Birmingham Mint Ltd.

Originally the firm had used hand and steam presses and coke fired furnaces making use of raw copper, zinc and a range of enamels. Today power presses, rolling mills, electric furnaces, machine tools, plating plant, steel, aluminium, copper, nickel and zinc are the order of the day to produce coins, blanks, tokens and medals.

By the opening years of the new millennium large orders for Euro blanks were being filled, contributing to the switch to a single currency in Europe, with the Birmingham Mint supplying its blanks to 65 percent of Europe's mints.

Above left: *An operator pouring a metal sample for analysis in the casting department.*
Centre: *A medal presented to employees of The Birmingham Mint Ltd to mark the commissioning of its new rolling mill.* ***Below left:*** *Inside the rolling mill.* ***Below right:*** *An interior view of the foyer.*

King George VI and Queen Elizabeth meet Birmingham dignitaries and their families during their visit in May 1948.

Acknowledgments

The publishers would like to thank
Birmingham Library Services

Thanks are also due to
Andrew Mitchell who penned the editorial text
and Steve Ainsworth and Judith Dennis for their copywriting skills